A TIME TO **PROFIT**

REAL STRATEGIES...
FROM TWO **REAL** WOMEN
CASHING-IN
ON **REAL** ESTATE

Andrea Weule

&

Gena Horiatis

Contents

Preface Nice to Meet You 4

Chapter 1 Discovering the New You: Basic Business Principles.. 17

Chapter 2 Assembling Your Support System: Power Team Members.. 27

Chapter 3 Building Blocks to Success: Wholesaling...... 38

Chapter 4 Endless Possibilities: Lease Options 72

Chapter 5 Expanding Your Strengths: Fix & Flip 85

Chapter 6 Uncover True Wealth and Prosperity: Buy and Hold... 100

Chapter 7 Compound Your Success: Turnkey Real Estate and Full Service Wholesaling 113

Chapter 8 Expanding Your Resources: Funding Your Deals 122

Chapter 9 Expose the Facts and Not Opinions: Market Conditions, Trends & Analysis 135

Chapter 10 Reveal the Lifestyle of Your Dreams: What's Your Niche? 147

Chapter 11 Unleash Your True Potential: Goal Setting. 156

Chapter 12 Welcome a New You: What's Next? 166

Epilogue Just Walk into the Sea 172

Dedicated to

My brother Phil Schatzka (1984 – 2016). Thank you for always being my biggest fan! *Andrea*

My husband Nick, who has exemplified Christ's love since the day we met. *Gena*

Nice to Meet You

"Why don't you start believing that no matter what you have or haven't done, that your best days are still out in front of you."
Joel Osteen

Where is the Real Estate Market Today?

My friends, we are in the perfect storm! In 2009, we were for all intents and purposes at the bottom of the market. In the years prior, home prices were escalating out of control. You could buy a house for $100,000 one month, do almost nothing to it, and sell it for maybe $125,000 the following month.

This went on for a number of years. People were speculating that it would continue this way forever. Well, that is, people who didn't have their hands on the pulse of the market. This frenzy was compounded by the fact that banks were giving out loans to anyone whose breath could fog a mirror. Crazy loans! Fifty years, interest only, nothing down. I might be exaggerating but not by much.

So what happened? Well, when we reached the top of the curve, a house purchased for $100,000 would sell for $200,000 a few years later to someone who never should have qualified for the loan. Then, seemingly overnight, the housing market crashed. We're not economists, but even we can make this profound observation. It was a sorry mess. Uninformed investors lost their skin and went running. Cash buyers became hard to find, though deals on properties were littering the streets like Bud Light cans after a Browns-Steelers game.

Worse yet, homeowners found themselves in serious trouble. That house they just paid $200,000 for was suddenly worth only $100,000 again. Hopelessness spread. People stopped making mortgage payments. Short sales become common, meaning houses were for sale and being sold with mortgages larger than the sales price. Banks foreclosed on homes in droves. Banks, which are not supposed to be in the real estate business, found themselves poorly equipped to handle the ensuing chaos.

This is now in the rearview mirror. Home prices have rebounded, faster and higher in some parts of the country than in others. Housing prices in areas like Los Angeles, Orlando, Dallas, Las Vegas, Phoenix, and Seattle have recovered greatly. In the more modestly priced areas of the country, the Midwest and South, the markets have been slower to recover, but it has and is happening.

What does this mean to you as an investor? In short, it's the best time in the history of your life to invest in real estate. Where to start? Start where you are: right in your backyard. There are deals to be had everywhere. We know this for a fact. Just check our frequent flyer mileage status. There are deals to be had all across North America, yet it is best for you to begin in your backyard. However, we want you to think of a very big backyard. Any place you can drive back and forth to in a weekend qualifies as backyard.

Your first few deals provide you the deepest learning experience if you can touch them, smell them, and suffer through them firsthand. Suffer? All things new tend to be a tad bit painful. It's good pain, though, like the way your muscles feel after a workout. Now, what's the best technique for your first deal? We recommend wholesaling. No money needed. No credit needed. As close to no risk as humanly possible.

Though you can wholesale properties anywhere in the real estate cycle, right now you can buy houses that will provide outstanding returns on your investment and hold them for passive income. Further, with the market recovery, you can buy houses,

5

renovate them, and resell them for a handsome profit. That was nearly impossible when we were hovering around the bottom. As markets continue to improve, speculative buyers are back. Some are choosing to buy properties with little to no positive cash flow, hold them for a few years, and then sell them for a large profit. The cycle will repeat. We strongly urge you, don't delay! Dive in now. The water is mighty fine!

"There can be as much value in the blink of an eye as in months of rational analysis."

Malcolm Gladwell

"Now, one thing I tell everyone is learn about real estate. Repeat after me: real estate provides the highest returns, the greatest values and the least risk."

Armstrong Williams

Gena Horiatis

 Out the window, the turquoise surf was playing with the rocks. The chatter of my family awaiting breakfast was filling my daydreams while I peeled mangos picked from a tree down the street on my early morning walk. Squeezing some local citrus onto the fruit plate, I wondered if we should go snorkeling or biking first. Big decisions of leisure. Two weeks with my loves – my four nearly grown children, a son-in-law, my son's girlfriend, and my precious husband. Fourteen days of paradise. How did I get here? Real estate profits paid for this escape. Flipping one home more than covered every penny needed.

The ultimate princess bride. What a stunning beauty! The gown was exquisite on her. Listening to the pianist play the song written just for Liz and her almost husband brought tears to my eyes. Married. How could it be? My little one. The food at the reception was mouthwatering. The cake beautiful and delicious. A private venue on the water - breathtaking. She had just graduated from a private university weeks earlier. Where did this money come from? How could we afford a wedding with all the costs of college tuition? Real estate profits. No stress. No more credit card bills. No more adding to the Home Equity Line of Credit. Just a couple real estate transactions.

I was walking this earth for some decades before I found real estate investing. In life, it always seemed like there were doors to walk through, so I walked through them. I grew up in a lower middle class family. My father was a carpenter. Winters in Cleveland are harsh, and I remember his nose and ears literally being purple when he'd get home. Mom would have a shot and a beer waiting to warm him up. My mother stayed home until Dad got sick, then she cleaned houses.

I grew up feeling like I wasn't entitled to anything, but I learned how to make my way. My mother would settle for nothing less than A's in school, so I figured out how to get them. Though I don't favor that version of parenting, I think it was a blessing to me. I adopted the Scripture, "And whatsoever ye do, do it heartily, as to the Lord, and not unto men." (Colossians 3:23) as my life motto and have, in fact, tried hard to pass it on to my children. With my modest but comfortable upbringing, I worked my way through Cleveland State University, taking the bus back and forth and working after classes at a record shop. Yes, records.

When I graduated from college with a teaching degree, there was an excess of teachers. I had only one interview for a teaching position for which I somehow showed up a day late. Needless to say, I didn't get the job. I like to think it was the Lord's way of putting me on another path. I ended up getting a position at IBM which was then in its glory days as "Big Blue." I moved from the position of secretary to systems engineer to marketing professional. Nothing in life is wasted. Some 25 years later, I marvel at how these old skills serve me.

I married an amazing man right out of college. Nick and I have been married now for 38 years. Our marriage gets better every year; we are crazy in love. When our children began arriving in our 30's, there was absolutely no question that I wanted to stay home. It was a financial sacrifice, but so worth it. Over a ten-year period, along came John, Liz, Grace, and Hannah. They are the joy of our lives.

Fast forward to age 54. I had been a stay-at-home mom for two decades and a piano teacher for one decade. Life has seasons. My husband had an excellent career, but with John and Liz in college at the same time and Liz's wedding on the calendar, I got off my pillow and wondered how I was going to create a noticeable amount of additional income. I had girlfriends my age scrambling to get a community college degree for medical coding and such, hoping to make $30,000 a year. Others were going to work in the local warehouse store or nursery. Would they gross $20,000 a year? I could renew my ancient teaching certificate and try to get a job pouring my life out and making barely enough to cover expenses.

In the summer of 2009 Dean Graziosi came into my family room – on an infomercial that is, corny as it sounds. He told me that this was the best time in history to make money investing in real estate. Who me? Only Donald Trump does that. Yet something in his eyes and in the tone of his voice convinced me to take a chance on the education offered. The rest, my friends, is history.

I started investing locally in the greater Seattle area. My very first deal, I made over $50,000. That was more than I earned in two of years of teaching piano! I did a handful of deals in Seattle before the higher returns of remote markets made sense to me. I ventured into the greater Cleveland, Ohio market. In my first year there, I accumulated ten cash flowing rentals. Now I continue to both hold properties for cash flow and flip homes for profit in several cities in the Midwest and South, along with wholesaling at home.

What I love is doing deals without using any of my own cash and hardly any of my own time. One of my favorite deals was brought to me by another investor in a suburb of Detroit. I found private funds from an investor in North Carolina. The guy in the Detroit area did all the work, and made about $6000 on the deal. The guy in North Carolina put in all the cash and made about $2000 on the deal. I coordinated a few emails, contracts and phone calls, and made about $17,000. Ah, that's a nice. Oh yeah, and I was in Hawaii while it was all happening.

In 2012 I was blessed and privileged to begin teaching investment strategies all over North America. Name the city, I've probably been there. I've even taught in Guam, New Zealand and Australia. It's been a whirlwind and a miraculous transformation for me. A re-creation of me, if you will. A baby boomer gone wild.

A couple years ago, I looked at my husband. He looked sad and worn out. His job was draining every spark of life out of him.

I got mad and determined to use real estate investing to free him from his job. I just needed to build a little more passive income. While I was busy at this mission, life happened. He lost the job that was consuming him. It was a classic blessing in disguise. Because of the income I had already created with real estate, my husband was able to take some down time. He rediscovered who he was and what he wanted to do. He exercised, learned to eat better and lost weight (so did I). He pursued his long buried passion for acting and was in plays, commercials, and even a made for TV movie! He laughed. Then for a short while, he took a lower stress job that allowed him the freedom to enjoy his family and continue to pursue his acting. Happily, this past year he left his job forever and is acting full time! What a delight! If this was the only thing I every accomplished in real estate, I'd say it was all worth it.

As I travel across America, I see a common scenario. Middle-aged women and men, young people, and retired seniors wondering what to do next. Where can they possibly go from their often overwhelming circumstances? Most have done their best. Like my husband and me, many attended college, got a job, and had babies. A lot of women put their careers on hold, thinking they would be able to step back into them many years later. But the world changes and so does life. Who is going to hire a 50+ year old woman who hasn't been in the work force for 20 years? What kind of job, let alone career, could such a person dare to believe is possible? May as well admit defeat and just go clean some houses.

There is an alternative. It's this creative and exciting world of real estate investing. No one can say you are too old or too young. No one can look down their nose at your resume. No one can say you don't have experience (Do you ever!). The game is played on your terms. You use your strengths and experiences. You create the rules. You run the team. It's time for the tip-off, and you have the home court advantage.

"Ask, and it shall be given you; seek and ye shall find;
knock, and it shall be opened unto you."

Matthew 7

Andrea Weule

I'm truly living the dream! I remember people saying "Living the Dream" when I moved to Denver and I thought I got it. I mean I had a job and a social life, but money was always a factor. A factor that I had limited control over due to the time and money constraints of a job. Now I have the ability to truly "lifestyle live". Not like in a Lifestyles of the Rich and Famous kind of live, but live how I choose. My husband loves baseball so we've been traveling across the US visiting all the major league baseball stadiums and rarely miss a playoff game, no matter where it's being played, if the St. Louis Cardinals are playing. I spend a week in Mexico with a girlfriend every year. I have taken my folks and in-laws on some great trips to include Hawaii, Disney World, NASCAR races, and even first class to an all-inclusive resort in Mexico. Even better - I take the summers off! I can still run my real estate business from home. I absolutely love for my kiddo and I to be able to go to the pool, visit museums and do art projects and experiments every day. Lifestyle living is about Living the Dream – and I'm doing it!

Of course, life didn't start this way. I grew up in a small town in Montana. I'd always been a busy person and involved in a lot of activities. I was a competitive swimmer all through school and participated in other activities - cross country, tennis, band, and even a little theater. My real passion and driver growing up was community service. I loved giving back and was volunteering for activities ranging from assisting with Special Olympic events to taking on the role of Governor for the Montana District of Key Club International.

After graduating from Montana State, I moved to Denver. I planned to give it three years and then head home if it wasn't working for me. Next thing I knew I was married to a wonderful man, Chip, and had an awesome kiddo, Caleb. I worked in the homebuilding industry in various positions including, superintendent, warranty general manager, and marketing and sales professional. Being in the building industry made the transition to real estate easier for me than it might have been otherwise, but I still made a lot of mistakes prior to education and support.

My initial venture into real estate investing was a struggle. I made poor decisions, trusted the wrong people, and got caught with my shorts down when the market took a dive. When I finally made the decision to invest in my education, I had to use my last available credit card (my husband and I were in debt more than $225,000 from investments gone wrong.) When your hole is that deep, you only have so many choices, and my choice was to dig deeper, get educated, and get to work. I did just that. In my first year as an educated investor I made a splash, but beyond earning money, I developed the tools to take control of my own destiny.

It was an awesome first year, we (my husband Chip and I) were able to make $4,400 on our very first deal by just helping out some friends that were upside down on their house. Our second deal was super creative. We used private money as our down payment and traditional financing for the purchase of two properties. These properties we then rented and did a cash out refinance. We were able to pull out enough cash to pay off the loan and the private money and still put $30,000 straight into our pocket! Later that same year we did a double closing that netted us $44,000 which was amazing. I've been nonstop since then – infected with the real estate bug.

Since then, I have completed numerous wholesale deals, rehabs, lease option deals, private money lending deals, and I own a number of rental properties. I continue to wholesale properties on a regular basis. I am always growing our retirement money through deals with other investor partners. Even though I live in Colorado, I have completed deals in eleven other states. I've taught others investment strategies across both the US and Canada. To go into a new community and give other like-minded people

13

the tools to improve their lives, the lives of their families, and their communities has been one of the greatest gifts of my life.

I worked hard for five years as an investor while still employed at my J.O.B. After we paid off the debt, took some great memorable trips, and built up our rental portfolio, I was able to leave my job and focus on real estate full-time. My goals have always been to work exceptionally hard on our business and grow our future.

Yes, I've been very successful financially. However real estate gave me an even bigger gift. I've been able to get back to the passions of my youth. I have the freedom and ability to volunteer more. I assist with programs here in Denver sending care packages to our troops overseas. I also work with programs that focus on the elderly and the youth in the Greater Denver Metro Area through the Volunteers of America. It is a wonderful feeling to be able to give back and make an impact.

The security and flexibility have been a gift that I've worked hard to achieve. I feel blessed to have the choice, yes my choice, to work for the first time in my life. Better yet, I'm only in my early 30's. Plus, I now have the ability to spend time with my family that would be missed if I was working a full-time job. We love to travel and look forward to the future when we can immerse ourselves in new cultures and communities across the globe. Why shouldn't we be away traveling and living in the many paradises this world has to offer? Real estate investing has been the tool to my success and is going to be the pension plan that no job today offers. Life is great!

"Whatever women do they must do twice as well as men to be thought half as good. Luckily, this is not difficult."

Charlotte Whitton

A Special Message from Our Hearts to Yours

This book is for everyone and anyone ready to learn proven skills to profit and transform your life with today's real estate market.

...The two paragraphs that follow are the only thing in this book exclusively for the ladies... ... ...

A myth clings to us like fog in the mountain. It has its frosty fingers around our necks. It chills our ambitions and puts our dreams on ice. The enemy buries our talents and gifts deep in the snow. But the sun is rising and your vision is thawing. You will not be held back. You cannot be stopped. You won't be denied.

The opportunities are too great to ignore any longer. The very core of your being is begging you to defrost. Meet men on the playing field head on. No one can do what you were made to do. Only you. Without you, there is a void. The arena of real estate investment needs you. You know how to do it all. You couldn't single-task if you tried. You are a multi-tasking Ninja warrior mama, and the market is calling you into the ring. Put on your pastel boxing gloves and step up.

"Women can do everything; men can do the rest."
Russian Proverb

Chapter 1

Discovering the New You:
Basic Business Principles

"The main thing is to keep the main thing the main thing."

Stephen Covey

 Many times gifts are dropped right in front of you. If you stepped forward, you would trip over them. Look down. There are some in your path now. If you have a teenager, you know they can walk over dirty laundry on the way to the hamper and never think to pick it up. Well, we have not quite outgrown that tendency ourselves. There are opportunities right behind doors and all you have to do is knock. If you knock, the door will open. If you trust enough to walk through it, you will find yourself in a new place. A nice place, but different. Being uncomfortable there doesn't mean you shouldn't be there. It just means you are growing. I don't believe my experience is unique. In fact, I believe that it's available to you today.

I was a stay-at-home mom for twenty some years when late one night I saw an infomercial telling me it was a great time to invest in real estate. So I tried it. It was one of a series of doors I chose to walk through. I didn't even have to hunt down the doors or use a GPS. They presented themselves to me. What made me unique is that I noticed the doors and had the courage to go through them. I trusted that if a door was put in my path, it must be for me. You have doors, too.

I guess I really shouldn't say I *tried* it, because if you decide to just "try" something, it's not going to work. You must decide to "do" not "try." I did and it worked. I had a little success, found another door, had a little more success, and found yet another door. I've walked through a succession of doors on my path to talking to you here.

I tend to think of this life transformation as a miracle – going from mother/housewife to professional real estate investor/mentor/teacher/speaker/author. In many ways it is true that things sometimes happen miraculously. But oftentimes miracles take our agreement and our effort. I've worked hard. I've

18

believed change was possible. It did take getting rid of some limiting beliefs. Even figuring out what my limiting beliefs were took a lot of digging and many months.

I used to be too old. Yep, used to be. Now I know I am EXACTLY THE RIGHT AGE for where the door leads. Otherwise, the door would be behind me, not in front of my face. I was afraid that I wasn't truly smart enough. Oh yeah, I'd fooled everyone so far, but just wait until they figured out how average I really am. Now, I'll shout it loudly: I am truly brilliant! (So are you.) I had this mixed-up belief that God would always provide what we needed but never an excess. Now I know that the Lord God Almighty, He who painted tropical fish with a thousand colors, wants to bestow extravagant riches on my life. Why? So I can do more good. Besides that, He loves me.

Do you see yourself in any of this? I'm guessing you do. Even if your story is quite different, you have beliefs that are holding you back. I'm going to ask you to do something. Leave those behind, even if you can't put words to them yet. Walk through the door. Trust me, you'll like it.

Many years ago, my best friend and I were walking our two young children in strollers when she said to me, "Gena, what are your personal goals?" I'm sure I stared at her dumbfounded because she began to giggle.

"What are you talking about?" I asked quite sincerely. "I have no personal goals. I'm raising my kids now."

If you are of a feminist bent, you may take this the wrong way. Please don't. In my life I've learned to be 100% involved and content in whatever I am doing. I wasn't longing to be in another place when I was bringing up my kids. I wasn't wishing away the days. I wasn't thinking of anything else. I was just doing my very best at the task at hand.

I am doing the exact same thing in this new chapter of my life called "Real Estate Investor." I have totally immersed myself in the new mission. Happily, this mission has extended to lending you a hand. Won't you take it? Focus and let's do this thing.

"Do what you can, with what you have, where you are."
Theodore Roosevelt

Points to Ponder and Discuss:

Think of a time in your life when an opportunity presented itself.

Did you take advantage of that opportunity?

If so, or if not, how did that make you feel?

Are there any opportunities in front of you at this very moment?

Are there any doors to be opened?

What are you choosing to do?

Can you identify a limiting belief?

What is it costing you to continue believing that way?

How can you change this belief to one that will empower you?

 I clearly remember being on the phone with a marketing guy who was selling me on the advantages of investing in real estate. "You are going to save a lot of money on your taxes."

"Huh, that's cool. Why?" I said naively.

"Because you are *starting a business.*"

"Oh. What on earth does that mean?" I wondered aloud. Apparently there was something called an entity under which my business would be run. I'd need some legal help in getting it set up. The entity had magical tax-saving powers. That's all I came away with from the initial pitch.

We all have to start somewhere, and that somewhere has to be where you presently are. Some of you are coming from a situation like me. As a long time stay-at-home-mom, I had little to no knowledge of how to operate a business or become a business person, and thereby how to treat this new pursuit of real estate investment *as a business.* Others of you are more like my friend Andrea. She was already in the business world, so this transition was less foreign. Either way, there are specifics to real estate investing that we all have to learn.

Let me emphasize. This is a business. If you are going to dabble in this the way you would try out a new spaghetti sauce recipe, stop now. If you are determined to make this work, as you would push forward even if your first batch of sauce was bad, then let's continue.

Chances are you are not an attorney or an accountant. This is not the time to pretend you are. You need to start your business correctly. One wise thing to do is to have an entity, probably an LLC (limited liability corporation), as your business structure. This will give you both asset protection and potential tax benefits. Use the services of an attorney for establishing your entity and get an accountant on your team who is knowledgeable about real estate investing.

You will need a checking account in the name of your entity. You have to be careful not to mingle funds. That's a big no-no at the IRS. I do not want to be the person to research all this. I always want to utilize the time and expertise of my team members. My job as a real estate investor is to make the deals. Period.

In terms of a business plan, I don't want you to get too bogged down here. This is all new to you. Start with your basic goals (see Chapter 11 on goal setting). Your business plan is going to grow out of your goals. It's easy to spend hours, days, and weeks creating your perfect business plan. The reality of it is, when you first start, you really don't have a clue. I suggest you spend no more than an hour outlining a business plan in your mind, and then start working on your deals. The plan will evolve as you find your place in this brave new world.

One thing that never occurred to me until I was attending an event at my real estate investment club is that I should have policies and procedures for my business. It seems insanely obvious now, but really, it never even occurred to me. However, much like a business plan, you can't really establish these in much detail until you get some experience. I'll give you an example of a procedure I have for purchasing a new property:

1. Inform the title company this will be a remote closing. Documents are to be emailed and sent back overnight.

2. Get wiring instructions for funds.

3. If private money lender, contact local attorney to draw up promissory note and mortgage.

4. Contact insurance company and get coverage.

5. Once email of documents is received, read carefully. Sign documents that do not require notarizing. Go to notary and sign those documents in front of notary as needed.

6. Go to Federal Express or UPS and overnight return documents.

7. Track closing progress with the title company.

8. Call utility companies.

Now, why is this important? Number one, you don't want to have to rethink this every time. It's easy in the rush of the moment to forget something important. Number two, you are building your business so you can sell it. What? You have no intention of selling your business. Well, at a minimum someone needs to be able to step in and run it for a few weeks while you are on a beach in the Caribbean. OK?

Policies, practices, and standards of operation: document what works and revise it over time.

It was quite the transition in my life to go from mom and wife to business mogul! It's hard for me to accept my new role as a reality. I'm an expert in real estate. There. I said it. And I mean it. But it was a long and winding road for me to really develop a business mindset, especially one that felt comfortable to me in my own head. You cannot be someone else, but you are leaving your old lifestyle behind. (Can I get an "Amen"?)

Be patient with yourself. Pay attention to what gets you excited in your new world. That's where you are going to be most successful. That's where to put your energy. Once you know where to focus, you will be better at treating it like a business because you believe in what you are doing. You have to be on guard with your emotions. This is not an emotional business; it's a numbers business. That doesn't mean we are nasty and cold-hearted. We help lots of people in the process of doing what we do, but our decisions and behavior have to be based on what the numbers say. I'll discuss that more in future chapters.

Financial freedom likely sums up what you are want. Is it possible? Is investing in real estate your answer? It can be. You are going to have to work hard, especially in the beginning. You are going to have to be persistent. You are going to have to pick yourself up and push hard when you really don't want to. You are going to fail a lot on the way to succeeding. This did not just fall in my lap, and it won't fall in yours either. You must struggle and strive. It will be worth it.

When I first started in real estate investing, we had two children in college at the same time and two more coming up close behind. We were increasing our home equity line of credit well beyond our comfort level even though we had saved for college. Then my eldest daughter announced that she was going to get married. We wanted to have a nice wedding for her. Where was all this money going to come from? Yes, the answer was real estate investing. I was able to contribute significantly to the college fund and pay for the wedding. A couple of years ago, real estate profits sent my immediate family of eight to Kauai for two weeks. My husband was able to say good-bye to his demanding and unfulfilling job to start a new career as an actor. This can be your golden ticket, but you are going to have to work it, sister!

"You cannot fly like an eagle with the wings of a wren."
William Henry Hudson

Building Momentum –

Here are Some To-Do's:

- Get an email account just for your real estate, preferably Gmail.

- Get a free Google voice number. See the following link: https://support.google.com/voice/answer/115061?hl=en&ref_topic=1707989

- Order business cards. www.vistaprint is one good place. Keep it simple. Just put your name, phone number, email and something that indicates you are a real estate investor, like "We Buy Houses. We Sell Homes."

- Create an affirmation that you repeat daily to keep your mindset where it needs to be! Here are a few ideas:

  "Every day I get better and better in every way."

  "I am in control of my destiny. I choose success."

  "Oh Lord God, Bless me indeed! Expand my boundaries so I can reach more for Your Kingdom. Keep your Hand upon me. Fill me with your Holy Spirit. Keep all things evil far from me."

Chapter 2

Assembling Your Support System: Power Team Members

"Snowflakes are one of nature's most fragile things, but just look what they can do when they stick together."
Vesta M. Kelly

Sometimes making a change in your life can be a lonely journey. You may even feel persecuted for having the courage to stand up and improve your circumstances. I actually lost a friend because I believed I could become successful in real estate. When I excitedly told her of my newfound passion and plans, she was so derogatory in tone and words, I determined never to talk to her about it again. When she asked me about it the next time, I simply said I wouldn't discuss it because she was discouraging to me. She begged, but I had to hold onto my convictions. The friendship was never the same. This can be sad, but there are sacrifices on the road to the Promised Land.

I encourage you to find ways to surround yourself with others who not only believe you can do this, but who are already successful in real estate investing. After all, this is a team sport. You will find networks of individuals who will support you and even partner with you in various ways. I'm a frequent visitor to www.deangraziosi.com. I had been chatting with another member on that site on and off for a couple of years. This guy was not pulling the trigger and one day he asked if he could just fund one of my deals. Could he? Yea, that works. You never know what treasures lay ahead just past the sacrifices.

Here are some great places to hang out:

www.deangraziosi.com and www.insiderelite.com

Facebook groups, LinkedIn groups, and above all your local real estate investment club are good choices, too. There you will find everyone you need for your business: cash buyers, private money investors, mortgage brokers, contractors, real estate attorneys, accountants, hard money lenders, even exterminators! Lots of great networking happens here, as well as inexpensive continuing education. You are never done learning! Make yourself known in the group. Just being visible and vocal gives you the aura of knowing what you are doing!

When I was new in this business I knew a lot more than I do now. Yep, thought I knew it all. I admit I tend to "ready, fire, aim." Many times that's the only way to get something going. However, there are other situations in which one should exhibit more caution. Legal matters fall into that category, specifically contracts. On my first several lease option arrangements, I ignorantly pulled contracts off the internet. I shudder to think about it now! Here's the story:

I put a responsible but struggling family into one of my renovated homes. The husband was receiving disability and the wife was supporting the family with a house cleaning business. They had three kids and a grandchild on the way. My heart went out to them. We met several times and discussed the way a lease option works. I have a clear and distinct memory of explaining that the option fee was not refundable should they not be able to exercise their option to purchase the home.

The term of the lease was two years. At the end of the two years, they still were not in a position to qualify for a loan. I extended the agreement an additional six months. At the end of the extension, they were no closer to qualifying. It did not make sound business sense to continue the arrangement. I let them know I would need to sell the house, and unfortunately this meant they had to move. Not surprisingly, they claimed to have no idea the option fee was not refundable and took legal action against me. My attorney did all he could, but my contracts were not worded correctly. What could have been avoided by a couple hundred dollars in legal fees in the beginning ended up costing me thousands.

Don't be pennywise and dollar foolish like I was. Use contracts for all your transactions and be sure that they are reviewed or created by a real estate attorney in your state.

Points to Ponder and Discuss:

You've heard it said that your family is the group of people you are born to but friends are the family you choose. Here's your opportunity to surround yourself with people who can help you achieve your dreams both personally and professionally.

Think back to a time when there was a door you could have walked through.

Did you let someone talk you out of stepping over the threshold?

How would your life be different if you had been surrounded by like-minded individuals? What can you do today in your current life circumstance to create a support circle?

Think of an achievement you have had in your life, big or small. How great was it or could it have been if you had people to celebrate with?

31

Power Team Members

 Ah, the mysterious POWER TEAM! Why on earth are we so attached to this idea? Believing you must have a power team is something that can hold you back. Since you don't have a clue what a power team is, who should be on it, or how you draft them, you may be perplexed and stuck. Maybe you will stall and do nothing because, after all, your power team isn't yet assembled. Well, just stop it now before you get started down this path.

Your power team, like your business plan, and even your goals, is something that is going to "naturally" evolve over time. It is not something you have to fully create before you begin.

You should start at the very beginning, a very good place to start. When we read we begin with A, B, C. When we invest, we begin with a real estate agent. Finding the right agent might take some doing, but that individual is the key to your success.

Real estate agents do not receive training in investing. They essentially learn how to use the Multiple Listing Service (MLS) contract and how to not get sued. It is your job to find the rare gem of an agent who understands and likes working with investors. Oftentimes, a good place to start is with Keller Williams or REMAX. Those particular offices usually provide at least a little training to their agents in the area of investments. However, I have often found a great agent at an office with only one location. This search is part of your great scavenger hunt! Here's what I want you to do.

How to Find a Real Estate Agent

Find a real estate office in the general area where you want to invest. Though any agent can show you any property, agents tend to know the neighborhoods surrounding their office best. The phone will likely be answered by an administrator.

The conversation is going to go something like this: "Hello, It's a wonderful day here at Keller Williams. This is Angie. How can I help you?" (Yes, they say something like that.)

"Hello Angie (use her name). This is Gena. I'm a real estate investor. I'd like to speak to one of your agents who works with investors." This will stop Angie from sending you to the agent covering the floor that day or the next one on her list. You are already in control. You know who you need to speak to, and you have said so. Sometimes Angie knows just what to do, other times she doesn't have a clue. In the latter case, ask to speak to the managing broker.

Once you get the investor-savvy agent on the phone, you need to verify that they do work with investors. "Hi Mike. This is Gena. Angie said you are the rock star agent for working with investors! Is that true?"

You are building rapport and taking the edge off the conversation. Who doesn't like to be a rock star? If Mike says that's him, you are off to the races. If not, ask for someone else, or call another office. Don't waste your time or Mike's time.

"So Mike, I'm looking for single family homes in safe, entry-level neighborhoods. I like three bedroom houses that are 1,000 to 1,500 square feet. I want to renovate these houses, put them back on the market (you can list them for me) and make a nice profit. Can you send me a couple dozen houses that are vacant, need work, and have had a price reduction or have longer than average days on market?"

Why are these points important? *Vacant* – someone is paying the bills and no one is living there. *Needs work* – a traditional home buyer wants a home ready to live in, not a project. *Price Reduction*

– the seller has started negotiating with himself. He's getting anxious. *Long days on market* – the longer the house sits, the higher the need to sell. In other words, these three characteristics define a *Highly Motivated Seller!*

This is not your all-inclusive conversation, but it will get you started. If Mike asks you questions you can't answer, (which neighborhoods? what price range?) you can rely on his expertise and have him tell you what his other investors prefer. How Mike performs will let you know if he's your guy. Sometimes you have to kiss a lot of frogs to find your prince, so pucker up!

Your real estate agent is your door to nearly everyone else you will need on your team. An agent who works with investors will know contractors, property managers, mortgage brokers, hard money lenders, everything you need! Referrals are always the best way to go.

The other key connection in building your team is your local real estate investment club. There are three websites you can use to find the clubs closest to you or your market. Search for real estate clubs on the following sites:

www.reiclub.com

www.creonline.com

www.meetup.com.

Visit every club you can drive to and mingle, mingle, mingle. Pick the one that suits you best and join it. Attend regularly. I have found my real estate attorney, contractors, mortgage broker, hard money lenders, private money lenders, and accountant at my local club meetings. Don't sell yourself short. Get involved with your club. If you have to drive an hour or two or three – it's worth it!

Let's talk a bit about some of the other members you will ultimately want on your team. It is advisable to start your real estate business as a wholesaler. We will fill you in on that in a later chapter. As a wholesaler, you are going to need to build a network of other investors, especially cash buyers. You will be learning how to be a "full service" wholesaler, so you will also want to be able to refer your buyers to contractors, property managers, and banks that can provide refinancing.

Adding a Contractor to Your Team

Contractors can be the bane of your existence or your guardian angels. Honestly, ladies (men you can eavesdrop here), have you ever had a hairdresser cut your hair for months or even years, and then suddenly, it's like they've never seen your head before and make a total disaster of your hair? I know you know what I'm talking about here. In my experience, contractors can be the same way. They do a house or two or three for you, then suddenly they drop the ball and leave your renovation an incomplete mess, and you are stuck paying for the problem with a replacement contractor. Just how do I know this? Been there, done that (a few times too many).

Please get your contractors on referral and check their references. Let them know up front you are going to 1099 them. Your accountant will be happy, and you will immediately sort out some of the less desirable ones. Always have your renovations bid by more than one contractor. It's too easy for even a great worker to get lazy and expensive when there is no competition. I struggle with this myself. I like to be loyal to my team, but business is business. Once your renovation is complete, it is important to get a Lien Waiver from your contractor. This document is verification from your contractor that his and all of his subcontractor invoices have been paid in full. This will help safeguard you from the possibility of future liens being put on your property.

Funding Sources

There are a lot of ways to get money for your deals and even techniques for doing deals that do not require any money, but it is a good idea to have a network of mortgage brokers, small community banks or credit unions, hard money lenders, and private lenders. Whether you use them yourself or refer them to your buyers, they will help you get deals done. Once again I recommend finding them at your local real estate investment club.

It's a Virtual World

Another source for finding key members of your power team is the wild Worldwide Web! This is a virtual world. You need to establish your presence out there. People do business with people they know, like, and trust, and lots of knowing, liking, and trusting happens online. Explore Facebook, YouTube, LinkedIn, and even Craigslist as you build your team.

No (wo)man is an island unto themselves. Real estate investing is most definitely a team sport! Batter up!

"I've learned that people will forget what you said, people will forget what you did, but people will never forget how you made them feel."

Maya Angelou

Building Momentum –

Here are Some To-Do's:

- Call and interview three or more real estate agents

- Get listings of potential investment properties

- Locate a Real Estate Investment (REI) Club and attend a meeting

- Exchange business cards with at least 20 people

- Ask for referrals. Make power team contacts

Chapter 3

Building Blocks to Success: Wholesaling

"Nothing in the world can take the place of persistence. Talent will not; nothing is more common than unsuccessful men of talent. Genius will not; unrewarded genius is a proverb. Education will not; the world is full of educated derelicts. Persistence and determination are omnipotent."

Calvin Coolidge

 My first deal was a simple bird dog deal, and most of the way through the deal my husband Chip and I didn't know what we were doing. We had decided to jump into real estate. Once we were at a barbeque with friends, and we told everyone there that we were becoming real estate investors. We didn't know what that meant at the time, but we were going to be real estate investors!

After the barbeque a couple of friends stopped us and asked if we could help them out. I said we'd be happy to try. The economy change had caused them to fall on some hard times, and they could no longer afford their home. They had taken great care of the home, and it was in a nice family neighborhood. I asked why they didn't just sell it with a Realtor. They said they owed about what the house was worth, so selling it in the slower market would cause them to have to bring money to the table at closing, something they couldn't and didn't want to do.

I went home and got online where I spent an hour or so on Craigslist. There was an ad saying "stop foreclosure" which gave me an idea. I sent emails to all of those types of ads and waited for responses. I received an email back from one that was quite promising, and he offered 10% of the profit. Pretty good if all we were doing was passing on our friends' information. However, we were in financial trouble of our own so the 10% was good for us, though not great. I explained to the guy that the deal was a really good one because the house was in a nice neighborhood, and the owners were motivated and willing to work with him. I then told him we needed 20% to offer him the contact information. He thought about it and agreed. We doubled our profit with just one request!

From there I introduced him to our friends. He signed paperwork with us and our friends and started the negotiating process with the bank. I honestly didn't have to do a thing after that. He handled everything. However, I did spend some time with him during the process, and I was able to learn a lot about how the short sale process works – think free internship and education. It took some time, but then we got the call that the deal had closed. We were presented with a check for $4,400; his profit was $22,000. Not a bad paycheck for helping out a friend and learning more about real estate!

Completing the first deal meant everything. That deal gave me the confidence to move forward and push through to success.

"Live out of your imagination, not your history."
                                                          Stephen Covey

 After a few deals, I got the hang of the assignment of contract and double closings. Then it was time to make some big money. The economy at the time was really hurting. Today it's better in most places. (That's the thing about real estate – it is always changing, ebbing and flowing like an ecosystem.) Due to the economic condition at the time, I saw an opportunity to go after some deals others wouldn't have considered.

I found a developer in Minnesota who had gone out of business and had a couple of unfinished projects. He had one project in particular that looked like it could be a home run. I was able to negotiate a short sale with the bank. Meaning the bank was willing to take a payoff short of (less than) what was owed. I locked up two end unit townhomes. The exteriors were completed on both of the units, but the inside spaces were just open shells. The interior units in the project had sold for more than $200,000, so that showed the potential value when they were completed.

Keep in mind that I was ready for big money but not necessarily big work. So my thought was to wholesale these units to a fix-and-flipper. Knowing the state of the economy and the amount of work these properties would require, not to mention the fact that I needed a discount so my buyer would be profitable, I had to get these locked up cheap. After some negotiating back and forth, I locked up each unit for $75,000.

Now it was time to get to work. These properties were located in Watertown, MN, which was a fairly long way from the Twin Cities. I did everything to find a buyer to the tune of about three months' worth of calls and emails, contacting Realtors and REI clubs. We did just about everything. Even when you get good at something, it still usually involves work and some struggles along the way. Finally, we had someone drive out to Watertown and put a "For Sale" sign in the yard.

Within a day of the sign going up, we received a call from a gentleman living around the block from the properties. He was a general contractor doing deals all across the US, and his father was a large scale real estate investor managing several projects around the US. This man had been curious about the townhomes when construction just stopped one day. The contractor was out of business, so there was no way of contacting him, nor did this man know who to contact at the bank. So he was excited by our sign and excited about the idea of having a project to work on near home.

There was a lot of back and forth negotiating for this property. We wanted to make a good profit, so we were hoping to sell each of the properties for $100,000 at a 50% or less ARV (After Repair Value) discount. However, his father was a savvy investor and wanted a good profit, as well. The buyer only wanted to pay $75,000 for each unit – which was what we had it locked up at. So that left us kinda stuck.

We went to the bank to see if they could wiggle at all on price. They knew all the challenges of this property, from the economy to the location to not qualifying for anything other than a construction loan in its current condition. That being said, they asked us how low we were thinking. I still wanted that $25,000 profit per unit so I asked for $50,000. I also told them we could close in two weeks to help sweeten their side of the deal. The bank discussed it and agreed to our request.

From there we got the two contracts in place along with the paperwork with the title company. We were able to close in ten days and walk away with a profit of over $43,000 after expenses. It was a "double double closing" that turned into a Home Run!

"Courage is fear that has said its prayers and decided to go forward anyway."

Joyce Meyer

Points to Ponder and Discuss:

Think back to a time in your life when you were able to help someone in a tough situation.

How did that make you feel?

Did this benefit you in any way?

Did you become stronger or more confident?

Have you ever felt your life was at a standstill or that you were in a rut?

What did you do to move forward?

Think about how much further you would like to grow. Don't limit your potential.

Is there someone in your life right now who you could reach out to?

Do you wish you had the opportunity to help in a bigger way? What can you do in your life right now that will enable you to make an impact in the world?

Wholesaling

Wholesaling is a simple concept that requires a lot of work upfront, but other than that requires no money, no credit, and my favorite, almost no risk. What a beautiful thing! So why doesn't everyone do it. Well there's that whole "hard work up front" issue. There is also the thing about being a human and assuming it has to be more complicated than it is. Not to mention that wholesaling requires a lot of rejection. Most of us are not tough enough to dust ourselves off and try again when we hear "No." It's been said many times that failure is a very real part of success, but a majority of people want to quit at the first sign of failure. Why? Because it's easier than being resilient and powering through the pain.

Okay, that's the pep talk. Now we'll tell you what wholesaling is. Wholesaling is truly as simple as getting a deal (or discount on a property) and selling that deal (still at a discount) to someone else. Here's an example that doesn't involve houses to help break it down. Let's say you're going to a sporting event, maybe a professional baseball game in the summer. Inside the ballpark, water sells for $5 a bottle. Outside the stadium there are vendors selling water bottles for $1 each. You can take these bottles into the ballpark as long as the seal is not broken. Obviously that's a great deal, so you spend your $5 on five bottles of water.

While you're enjoying the game, the person next to you complains about the heat, the fact that he has to miss the game to get a bottle of water at the concession stand, and the fact that it will cost $5 for a bottle of water. Being the nice person that you are, you offer the sports fan a couple of bottles of your water for half the price. He can have two bottles right now, while still in his seat, for the $5 he would have spent at the concession stand. He gladly accepts your offer because, once again, it is obviously a great deal. How cool is that?

You've just wholesaled water. Yes, that's right; you got a deal on the water yourself and then sold it to someone else for a deal. You've passed along the deal and still had three bottles of water to enjoy during the game free and clear.

Well that was a simple example, and to be honest, wholesaling real estate is just that simple. As I mentioned above, it does take a fair amount of work up front. Find people that want houses. Find people that need to get out of their houses. Put these people together using one of a few methods mentioned and you'll make money. The more motivated they both are the better off you'll be in getting a deal.

Okay, so let's roll into the parties involved in a wholesale deal. This is as simple as ABC. First there is the motivated seller. We'll call them A in the ABC transaction. This person needs to get out of their home for one reason or another. The next person is you, the savvy investor (wholesaler). We'll call you B in the ABC transaction. Lastly there is the cash buyer investor who is looking for a good deal. We'll call them C in the ABC transaction. They are looking for their next rental property or their next fix-and-flip deal.

So let's explore the motivated seller a little more. A motivated seller is someone who needs to sell their home quickly. This can be due to health issues, divorce, death, job loss, job relocation, or a number of other factors. Time is usually a large factor for these sellers. The longer they have to wait to find the right buyer the more the expenses begin to pile up. Additionally, their homes oftentimes need repairs or updates that may prevent a retail buyer from purchasing the home. This again creates a great opportunity for the right wholesaler to lock up a good deal.

Now let's take a look at the cash buyers looking for deals. As I previously mentioned, they are usually looking for another rental property or for a fix-and-flip project. So you may ask, "If they are already investors, why don't they just find their next deal themselves?" Great question! Well, as I mentioned, finding a great deal is a lot of work and can take time. Their skill set is usually in managing their rental properties or fixing a home and making it beautiful for a retail buyer. If you can find them their next project, then they can focus on what they are good at. Over the years, I've purchased many homes from wholesalers. I've been able to focus on growing my rental portfolio while others bring me my next property.

Really it comes down to filling two buckets: motivated sellers and cash buyers. The more you put in the buckets the more money you can make. Now comes the age old question, "What came first: the chicken or the egg?" Well with wholesaling it is often what should you get first, buyers or deals? To be honest, you need both and should focus on both. If you get buyers first, you'll have a better idea of what they want in a deal. If you know what they want, then you will have better focus on the homes and areas to go after. However, if you start looking at properties and making offers, you'll be able to communicate with buyers. Also buyers will take you more seriously if you are actively looking at properties and negotiating deals. Either way, no matter your approach, you need to do it with purpose.

Take action, don't just be busy. If you're going to look at homes, make offers on the homes you see. If you're going to contact buyers, find out specifics on what the buyers want.

Personally, if you are brand new to real estate you should start with buyers. If you have a buyer's criteria then you'll have a direction to proceed. Also, in addition to the focus on where to look, you'll have the confidence to make offers knowing you'll have a buyer if the offer is accepted. The best thing you can do is to start networking. Find people who are investing in real estate in your local market.

Where to Find Buyers

Real Estate Investment Clubs

Find a real estate investment club to attend. Who do you think belongs to real estate investment clubs? That's right, real estate investors. So this is a great place to actually meet cash buyers face-to-face. I enjoy meeting buyers in person, and I've found it is an easier way to talk to them about what they want in a deal. A great way to find true investors is to ask the person working the front door to point out those currently doing deals.

So how do you talk to a cash buyer to get their criteria? First I start by asking what they are finding right now in the market. It is a very open-ended question, and I know I'll probably get a vague or generic answer, but that's okay. At least I've broken the ice. From there I tell them I'm a wholesaler in the area and would love to find them their next deal. I always say that I know it isn't easy to find the right deals, but I'm willing to work hard and put in the time and effort to secure the right deal for them. Hard work is something that will always be respected.

From there I ask them what they want in an investment deal. Again I know I'll get a vague answer, but it opens the door for me to ask follow-up questions. Next I ask them if they would mind telling me about the last successful deal they completed. This is great because it allows them to brag a little about their success, and if I listen closely I'll get their criteria as they describe the deal, including price, size, area, style, etc. Another major consideration is what strategy they use for investing. Do they like rentals, fix-and-flips, or lease option strategies?

From there I like to let them know I'm serious and actually playing the game. I tell them about "a deal I checked out the other day" or "a deal I'm currently negotiating." If I've made an offer, I'm negotiating. After I've painted a picture of the deal, I ask if they would be interested if I do get it locked up. If yes, great, I have a good feel for their criteria. If no, I need to follow up and find out why they are not attracted to the deal. That will help me narrow down their criteria.

You can attend local and regional foreclosure auctions to see if any of the people buying homes there are looking for other properties. Get there early and, if at all possible, have a list of the homes they will be bidding on. Pay attention to who is there and watch as the auction takes place. Take note of who bid on what house and up to what price. That information is golden. If they bid on a specific address, you can look up the details of that home later (i.e. beds, baths, square footage, and then look at the neighborhood online). If they bid up to a certain point, then you know what they are looking for and how much they are willing to spend on another home in that area later.

After the auction is over, you go to work. Knowing that the guy in the red polo shirt bid on three houses and got one doesn't do you much good unless you can talk to him and get his contact information. Once you have his contact information, you can add it to his home criteria. Ask him if he would be interested in any deals you bring to him that are as good if not better than the one he got or the ones he offered on. Once again, buyers at auctions need cash, and if they are there bidding you've qualified them as a cash buyer by the environment alone.

Landlord Buyers

You can start by emailing and calling all landlords in your area. Find out if they are looking for additional properties. If they know the power of a good rental, they may be interested in more rentals but not know how to go about finding their next deal. So start by looking for rental ads on Craigslist and locate "For Rent" signs.

If you can get a phone number or email, reach out to the owner. Ask them how their rental is treating them. Find out if they'd be interested in getting more rental properties. Ask them the specifics on their rental as you did in your discussion at the REI club. Find out what area of town interests them, their cash flow amount, if they can handle repairs, and what return on investment they are looking for. Once you have their criteria, you can go after another round of properties for this landlord cash buyer.

If individuals are already buying houses in your market with cash, then why shouldn't they be buying properties from you? This is a great way to get good buyers and qualified buyers, since the best way to qualify a buyer is the proof that they've been able to close on other deals with cash. Also, these closings can give you all the information you need regarding their criteria. If they bought a three bedroom, two bath, ranch style home in the University area for $75,000, then there is a good chance they may want to buy another one just like it. You go find it for them.

Okay, so where do you get this magical list of cash buyers? You can get a real estate agent or title company to pull a list of all properties in the last six months that closed cash (meaning there was no mortgage in place). Send a letter to these people and see if they would be interested in additional properties. Introduce yourself as an investor in the local market who works hard to find discounted properties. Mention that you saw that they bought (list the address) and you'd love to help them find similar deals. If they are interested in discounted properties, they should give you a call. Make sure they have your email and phone number. Let them come to you.

Advertising Your Deals

If you've been out looking at properties, then you've got a good idea of what is on the market. Use that knowledge to attract buyers. This can be done online via www.craigslist.org or another free classified site or on bandit signs and flyers in your local community. You have two options:

1. You can create a ghost ad (something you make up) for a property that you have created. Now this property should have the aspects of homes common in the area. Also, you need to use key words that will attract a buyer including "needs work," "handyman special," "motivated seller," "this deal won't last long," "cash buyers only," "attention investors," etc. Finally, you want to make sure the property is listed at a good price. I always recommend shooting for about two-thirds of the ARV (After Repair Value) of the property. That way it is discounted but it isn't such a great deal that you'll never be able to find a property at that price in reality. You need a carrot, but make sure the carrot is something you'll be able to duplicate.

2. Nothing attracts buyers more than a good deal. If you have a good deal, put it out there for buyers to see. Go ahead and place an ad for the property if you've got it locked up. I often do this with properties even after I've gotten a buyer for it. Might as well use the good deal to attract future buyers for my next deal.

Social Media

My husband always says, "We live in the future." It is so true. With technology at our fingertips, it is so easy to meet and communicate with people today. So why not use those creative options to build your buyers list. Use networks such as LinkedIn, Facebook, and even YouTube to help network with other investors out there. Go to any of these mediums and search for Real Estate Investors, Investment Group, Real Estate Networks, or Cash Flow. The possibilities are endless. Sign up, log in, search, join, and start connecting. A large majority of this business is networking, so start making connections today!

 **If finding buyers seems unreal, like unicorns in rainbows, please watch a special video we created for you.**

Go to www.atimetoprofit.com/learn

Where to Find Motivated Sellers

You have two main approaches for finding deals from motivated sellers. The first and most common is by making offers on properties on the MLS (Multiple Listing Service). The second is through your own marketing channels looking for properties for sale by owner (FSBO's). Regardless of how you go about getting the deals, you'll want to make sure the seller is truly motivated. As stated before, the more motivated they are the better chance you have of securing a good deal.

Here are a few factors that will help you determine their motivation:

1. The property needs work – either repairs or updating throughout the house. If the house is not in move-in-ready shape, your retail buyer competition decreases, so the seller will be more interested in your offer.

2. The price of the home has been reduced or the seller has stated "bring all offers." If they've started negotiating with themselves, then they may be more open to your offer.

3. The home has been on the market for a long period of time. Anytime a home has been on the market for more than 30 days, the more motivated the seller will be and the more willing to take your offer.

4. The home is sitting vacant. If no one is getting the benefits of living in the home then the seller will be more open to selling at a discounted price. Over time bills and expenses will add up for an empty home.

How to Find Properties Using Your Real Estate Agent

First, as we mentioned in Chapter 2 (Power Teams), you have to find a good agent. I have four main criteria for my agent. They must be:

1. Open-minded

2. Creative

3. Hard-working

If they have these traits and are willing to work with me, I'm set. Also, number 4, I have to like my agent. The more I like them, the better chance I have to continue to work with them. I am willing to call them more and that usually leads to more offers. So find one that fits your personality and your strategy!

It is key to let the agent know right up front that you want to make a lot of offers. I always start by telling agents that yes, I'm an investor. I don't start out by saying I'm going to wholesale. I state, "I buy houses one of three ways...1. I buy fix and resell for a profit, 2. I buy fix and rent for cash flow, or 3. I sometimes quick flip to other investors." That way I let them know I'm a wholesaler without putting a big sign out there saying "I'm a wholesaler."

Wholesaling has picked up a negative connotation over the years because many wholesalers never follow through and close deals, so some Realtors do not like working with them. Sometimes, in my first or second conversation with an agent, I tell them I'll need them to make 10 offers a week for me. This is because, in reality, you'll have to make a lot of offers to get those great deals. Stating this upfront can weed out some Realtors before I get too invested in working with them.

Okay, next let's talk about your contingencies. If you walk away from a deal, you only have to do that once, so you only need one contingency. Some wholesale investors use the contingency "pending my partner's approval." This means that if my end buyer doesn't like the property, I have an exit. I personally do not use the partner's approval since it can be a bit of a red flag. I've had many Realtors say that they won't consider my offer until my partner has checked it out. I do use an Inspection clause because it is common. It is so common, in fact, that everyone (investors and retail home buyers) use an inspection clause. One thing you could do is to shorten the time frame. I sometimes will do 10 or even 7 days to help make my offers more attractive. If I've got a good buyers list, however, that shouldn't be a problem.

Additionally, I follow up by telling the Realtor that I want to make this easier for all parties involved by creating a template for the offers. This will save both of us time. First they send me listings which I review and send back to them with offer amounts. For the first offers I've usually met them in their office and gone through their Board of Realtors' sales contract and added my terms and contingencies to it. Once we have a finalized contact, we can copy and use it over and over again. The only thing that will change for my offers is the date, seller name, address, and offer price. I've also given them copies of a blank earnest money check and a proof of funds letter (covered later in this chapter). This template system allows them to make each offer in less than five minutes, which helps eliminate some of the burn out on their part.

Finally, I search for Realtors through a website called ActiveRain.com. It is a social media site for Realtors. I do not use the search box at the top (that is for searching properties). Instead I click on the Search button and type in Area and the word Investor (i.e. Los Angeles, CA Investor). I don't have to put anything in there for Real Estate since it is a Real Estate website. Now you'll get tons of responses and several will be news articles and blogs. You are looking for Profile pages which will be listed like this: activerain.com/jdoe. Just a slash with their profile name. Email a handful of these responding Realtors a basic description of what you want them to do and see who writes back. If you email ten, you might only hear from two, but that eliminates eight calls and can save you some time.

How to Find Deals Not on the Market

Market directly to homeowners looking for the few "motivated" sellers who will eventually bring in the paychecks. There are three things I know about marketing:

1. It works. Without marketing I don't get any leads, hence no deals and I don't make any money.

2. I need to be consistent. Without consistency my marketing is not effective, and if I'm not effective then I don't get any leads. No deals, no money.

3. Marketing means a lot of trial and error. This means it is difficult, scary, and frustrating. But I hate the alternatives worse. So, gradually I have learned to respect marketing.

Methods of Marketing

Direct Mail

This is our top producer, and it works well with the downside that it can be expensive. In my experience and opinion, mailing to homeowners is more about the target than the message. If I send postcards to a pre-foreclosure list, I have to wonder how many pieces of mail these homeowners get. Probably a metric ton! Everybody and their brother is sending mail to these folks telling them they will buy their house.

As I see it, you have two choices: either offer something so special and unique in your message that your letter or postcard floats to the top of the stack or be consistent in your "repeat" mailings, thus having your mail at the top of the stack most of the time. I think it is more about having your message in front of the homeowner on the day they finally decide to solve their problem. If you are going to start a direct mail campaign, I suggest multiple touches, say three to five times each. In today's culture of information bombardment, you may need more contact before they trust you enough to respond.

Newspaper Ads

These are something I used to do when I first started but not so much now. If you target the Denver Post, it could get a little (read *a lot*) spendy, but if you target the smaller local papers it can be pretty reasonable. Something you may also want to do is call on FSBO and For Rent Ads in these same papers and perhaps you can scoop up some deals that way. This is actually a pretty good way of getting Sandwich Lease Option deals (owner financing-type deals with low equity but good monthly cash flows and a nice option fee, covered in a later chapter).

Real Estate Agents

I have heard that agents can be a decent way to find deals. I am less likely to have Realtors help me find deals to specifically wholesale. However, I have found that the deals I get from Realtors are usually deals that have gone bad. Also, I have not had much luck with Realtors in a "good or tight" market, as is the case right now in Colorado, with the exception of when a deal goes bad. Still, they are a resource, so get the word out to all the Realtors in your database and let them know you can close with cash in as little as three to five days without any contingencies.

When a Realtor has a deal that blows up a few days before closing, you want to be the guy or gal they call. I have landed more deals like this from Realtors than I have in working with Realtors to actually find me a deal in the traditional manner. Finally, a huge bonus for having a Realtor on your power team is that they can pull comparable sold home information for you so you are able to establish an After Repair Value (ARV) for your properties. It is extremely helpful to know the current selling prices for homes in move-in condition and similar to your home.

Referrals

These are great, and for the most part they are the cheapest leads you can find. There are many ways to play the referral card.

- Let everyone, and I mean everyone, you come in contact with know that you buy real estate with cash and close quickly, and you are also "way good" at solving real estate-related problems.

- Find other "bird dogs" to get the word out on your behalf, and pay them a marketing fee.

- Have a meet up workshop or build a website that trains your bird dogs, making them more effective through education.

- Business groups, church groups, singles groups, Boy Scout & Girl Scout groups, sporting groups, networking groups...let them all know who you are and what you do. Make it clear that you pay referral fees.

Wholesalers

If you have a good buyers list or are building one, then you may be in a position to find a buyer for another wholesaler's deal and get a fee. Another way to look at this is that if you are great at finding deals you should team up with another wholesaler who has a strong buyers list. This is yet another great way to get paid.

Bandit Signs

Yes, using these signs can be a crazy experience. They are a pain to put out. They cost money, and you get the weirdest calls. They also just happen to work. They are frowned upon by the local authorities, and they are called "bandit" signs for a reason. They generate copious amounts of calls in some markets, less in others. The good thing is that I am just looking for one call, the right call, the motivated seller call. This is such grass roots marketing that lots of folks skip it because they think it won't work. Don't be one of those folks.

Get yourself yellow corrugated plastic signs 18" x 24" and wire stakes. One good source for these is signwarehouse.com. Put out at least 18 signs in any given neighborhood in areas of heavy, slow-moving traffic. I suggest you don't use your personal cell phone on these signs, but use something like a free Google voice number with your local area code. My favorite sign is "We Buy Houses/Any Condition/xxx-xxx-xxxx". You will get calls from sellers as well as cash buyers. Track your marketing success by always asking where your sign was seen. Place bandit signs regularly and reap the reward of leads.

Here is my suggestion for your best starting point: begin with your Realtor. This will eliminate a lot of the stress of making offers for the first time. They can help you with the paperwork and all other aspects of getting your first offers out there. Then once you've gotten a little more comfortable, start marketing "directly" to homeowners in some fashion, be it referrals, bandit signs or cold calling the newspapers and Craigslist. I have had far better success over the years with this approach than picking through the MLS, but hey, that's just me. If you want to be successful, go find the deals or you could be waiting a long time for the deals to find you.

Could you use more clarity on finding sellers? Sometimes sharing in a visual format clears things up!

Go   to www.atimetoprofit.com/learn

The Strategies

Bird Dog/Property Locator/Property Finder

This is the simplest form of wholesaling and also the easiest. Bird dogs or property locators simply go out and find potential leads for other investors and are paid for their efforts. I recommend that if you want to be a bird dog, you start out by finding out what other investors want. Once you have their criteria, you go out and find a similar deal. The one caveat here is that these cannot be listed (MLS) properties. If they are on the market, unless you have some secret inside information, you really cannot bird dog them. So find a property from a For Sale by Owner (FSBO). Make sure you find out about the deal. Are they motivated? Once again you want to get the story. You do not have to negotiate the deal, but make sure there is potential for a deal or you'll be wasting your buyer's time, which won't make them want more deals from you.

Once you have a "like" property, let your buyer know about the deal. I recommend you describe the deal to the buyer and see if they are interested. Do not disclose the address until they are on board. You can use a simple bird dog agreement to secure your fee in the deal. Personally, I use a marketing invoice, such as a simple Microsoft word invoice template, and I ask them to sign the agreement.

58

Once we have an agreement in place, I'll give the buyer the seller's contact information. I also want to ensure that if they close, I'll get paid. The best way to do this is to follow up with your buyer every few weeks to check on the deal. Remind them that you brought them the deal. Also, I find out what title company or attorney my buyer uses and make sure I send a copy of the signed agreement or invoice to them. That way, when the deal closes, the title company will already be in possession of the agreement.

To put a bird dog deal simply, you are selling information. You're selling the potential deal, the lead to a buyer, so they may be able to make money on the deal. You're selling the information commodity they do not have without you.

Assignment of Contract

My favorite strategy is the Assignment of Contract. I like it because it is also quite easy, and there are not too many moving parts. Once again, I like to start by finding out what my buyers want. If I know what they want in a property, then I know what a good deal looks like for them and where to find the deal. I can do this by making offers to FSBO's, or I can use my Realtor to make offers on like properties on the MLS. To ensure that my contract will be assignable, I always note in the contract that it is assignable (some states have a section on assignability right in the contract). If there isn't a section in the contract, then behind my name or company name as the buyer I add "and/or assigns."

Once I get an offer accepted, I can present the deal to my buyers. This is a lot less complicated in that I have the property locked up under contract, so I can freely advertise the deal to my buyers. The key is that I want to advertise the property at the wholesale price (the price that I have it locked up for plus the profit I want to make).

When you have a buyer who agrees to the wholesale price, you present them with the original purchase contract and an assignment of contract. The assignment of contract has two main parts. 1. You as the assignor, give up all rights to the initial purchase agreement in exchange for money. 2. Your buyer, the assignee, agrees to fulfill all the terms and contingencies of the contract. From here you make sure the closing agent gets copies of both agreements, and you get paid at closing.

To put an Assignment of Contract simply, you are selling your equitable rights to the deal. You, as the buyer on the original contract, are selling your rights to the deal. So really you're selling the contract or the paper rights to the deal.

Double Closing

Double closings (aka simultaneous closings or same day closings) are a great option for deals that are not assignable because they are owned by a bank (Real Estate Owned, or REO property), are a short sale, or are a deal you've locked up that will allow you to make a very large profit. This is a great option because it allows you to wholesale without having to disclose the fact that it is a wholesale deal or what profit you are making. Now be aware that in most areas this will be public record after the closing, but it is not transparent up to and during closing. This sounds good. How does it work?

It starts out the same as an assignment of contract. First find out what your buyers want so you can go after the right deals. Second, get a property locked up. Once again this can be done via FSBO's or the MLS with your Realtor. On this contract you are the buyer.

Once you have a property locked up, you advertise it to your cash buyers at the new higher price. This is where it can get a little more complicated. You have to take into account some additional fees. You will actually be purchasing this property, so you'll have two sets of closing costs. For a quick estimate I often use 3% of the buyer's wholesale price. This will usually cover both ends, as many of the fees (including the title search) only have to be paid once. Talk to an investor-friendly title company or attorney for a clearer estimate. Most title companies require you to fund your end of the deal prior to closing on the second, requiring transactional funds. This fee can vary by lender and can range from $1,000 to $5,000. Get referrals for transaction lenders at your local real estate investment club. This will be an additional fee as well. Make sure you take this into account.

The new price you advertise to your buyers must include the price you have it locked up for, plus the additional fees, and most of all, the profit you want to make. Once you have a buyer in place, you then need to fill out a second purchase agreement. On this contract you're the seller and your cash investor is the buyer. Once both contracts are locked up, you submit them to the title company. If you have to request transactional funds, you can do it at this point. You'll have to sign two sets of closing documents and can collect the cash profit at the time of closing.

To put a double closing simply, you are actually purchasing and closing on the property from your seller. Then you are selling and closing the property with your cash buyer. It is a same day closing, but in this scenario you are selling the house.

Selling an LLC

This is a great option if you cannot do an assignment of contract and do not want to do a double closing. The concept is almost the same as the assignment of contract. However, instead of assigning the rights to the purchase agreement to your buyer, you assign the rights to the company that has the contract locked up.

Once you have a buyer and their criteria, you can start looking for properties. I recommend when you make an offer using this strategy, you set up a new LLC in which to make the offer. You can usually do this by applying for a new LLC via your state's Secretary of State website. Remember that there will be costs associated with this as well. However, they vary by state and are often less than the fees of a double closing. This should not be the main company you are using to do real estate business. This is a company you are using to wholesale this particular property. Once this LLC is sold, you will create another.

Once you have a property under contract that is non-assignable, you put the deal out to your buyers utilizing this LLC. Advertise it at the wholesale price and find the right buyer. When you have a buyer lined up, use a contract or even a simple invoice to sell the LLC to the buyer. The amount for the LLC sale is the amount of your profit. Once the new buyer is the owner of the LLC, they can freely close on the property.

The other main document the new buyer may need is an operating agreement of the LLC showing they are now the rightful owner of the company that has the rights to close on the contract. This is a great, creative way to make a wholesale fee on a non-assignable property without having to double close and pay the additional fees.

To put selling an LLC simply, you are selling a company that has the rights to close on a property under contract.

Wholesaling strategies can seem a little confusing at first; we made a video to further explain.

Go to www.atimetoprofit.com/learn

How are you going to get a deal? How do you know if it is a good deal? This is where having a buyers list and knowing what they want comes in handy. You'll know what your model needs to be. Also, knowing your market (to be covered in Chapter 9) will help you determine the discount needed for a good deal. You need two main things for a house:

1. The ARV (After Repair Value) for the subject property.

2. The estimated repair amount to get the property in move-in ready condition. What needs to be done to get a retail buyer or renter to move into this home and how much will that cost?

To find comparables (or "comps") you need to make sure you are dealing with like properties. Like properties must be:

- SOLD homes in the last three to six months
- In the same area - within a half mile radius
- Of the same style - ranch or two story or split level
- Have the same number of bedrooms and bathrooms
- Have similar square footage +/- 20%
- Similar in age +/- 30 years

To find the ARV, take average comparables by $/square foot, and then multiply by your house's square footage to determine the After Repair Value.

To determine repair costs, estimate the Price per Square Foot ($/sq ft) for the repairs and multiply by the square footage of the home. I use an average amount to determine my repair costs. The reason I do this is that I do not have time to walk through and take note of every little outlet, light fixture, or tile that needs to be replaced. I like to spend very little time, especially if I have a very small chance of my offer being accepted.

Here are the estimates that I use. (Note: Compare these estimates with your local market by visiting your local home improvement store or discussing repair estimates with your buyers. Also note, these numbers could double in higher priced markets.)

- Light (Cosmetic) Rehab = $5-$15/sq ft

  Includes cleaning, painting, flooring, appliances, light fixtures, fans, plugs and switches

- Medium (Update) Rehab = $15-$25/sq ft

  Includes all items in the light rehab, plus updating bathrooms, kitchen, doors and windows

- Heavy (Extensive) Rehab = $25-$40/sq ft

  Includes all items in the light and medium rehab plus repairing structural issues and updating mechanicals (electrical, plumbing, HVAC)

If you have anything beyond these types of rehabs, make sure that your buyers can handle major work.

Now that we have the ARV and you have an estimated repair amount, the only other thing you need is to take into account the discount your buyers desire. The formula is as simple as this: take the ARV, remove the discount, subtract the repairs and you will have your wholesale price. Now subtract the profit you want. Here's how it works:

Wholesale Numbers
ARV x Desired Discount (cents/$) = Buyers Discount
Subtract Repairs ($/square foot x sq ft of the Property)
= Wholesale Price (Price your Investor Buyer Pays)
Subtract the Profit Amount you Want for the Deal)
Subtract Additional Costs if not Able to Assign

= Maximum Allowable Offer (MAO) – maximum amount of your offer

Here's an example:

Let's say your calculated ARV is $100,000 and your buyer wants a 25% discount or 75 cents/$ less repairs. The repair estimate is $15/square foot. (The home is 1500 square feet so that's a repair estimate of $22,500.) Finally, you want a $5,000 profit.

It will look like this:

ARV =	$100,000
Discount x .75 =	$75,000
Repairs	- $22,500
Wholesale Price =	$52,500
Your Profit	- $5,000
MAO	= $47,500

Make sure it is a good deal for your buyer. Sometimes you'll run the numbers based on your buyer's criteria, and the offer amount will be higher than the list price.

In a competitive market, there will likely be multiple offers on a property, but this can still work. In the case of multiple offers, a seller will often call for Highest and Best. This means that each buyer will resubmit their strongest final offer.

If you are in a slower market, you will need to make an offer much lower than list price so that your wholesale price is still less than the list price (often much less).

Most buyers will check out the property online and will see the list price. They will expect you to have negotiated a deal to get them excited.

 If the numbers are making your head spin, we've got relief.

Go to www.atimetoprofit.com/learn

How to Make an Offer

Now we've got what we need to make an offer. We have a motivated seller. We've run the numbers. Next we need the paperwork to make it happen. First you'll need a Real Estate Contract to purchase property. This is a major reason I recommend that you start making offers through your real estate agent. This can relieve a lot of the pressure and confusion of making offers. Follow the same steps we talked about in the Power Team chapter (Chapter 2) and also previously here in the Wholesaling chapter. In addition to a contract, you'll need earnest money and a proof of funds letter. Here are some options on how to handle these.

Earnest Money

Earnest money is often one of the biggest stumbling blocks for new investors with limited cash resources. I'm going to give you four ways to eliminate the earnest money obstacle.

Get earnest money from your buyers. You need to really sell yourself and create urgency with your buyers. Tell them you are certain you can find them their next deal, but to secure the deal you need to have earnest money from them so you can lock it up. Just work out a simple agreement between the two of you to secure the money. Also, if they work with a specific title company, you can have them put the earnest money in an escrow account that you can reference when you make the offer.

Use a promissory note. This is a great option as long as you don't push the envelope too far. This is a simple promissory note that says you'll pay the earnest money at a later date. I recommend you do not extend the time period too far. When I use this method, I only extend the time period to the end of the inspection period. If you find a buyer, they can put the earnest money down. If you do not find a buyer, you can exit the contract prior to the end of your time period without ever having to put money down.

Write a check made out to "Title" (yes, that's it). Fill in the average earnest money amount most common in your area. Make a photocopy and have your agent use the copy to submit offers. The reality is that many of your offers are not going to be accepted, but you need to check this box to get your offer even looked at. Also, if you think about it, does anyone actually hand deliver the contract and checks anymore? The answer is no.

I always laugh when I'm watching HGTV's Property Virgins and Sandra gets her clients to sign the contract and then says she'll deliver it to the sellers and see what they say. Really? No, the agent is going to fax or scan and email it over to their listing agent. So the check is only going to be a copy or electronic version anyway. Also the check will only be cashed if the offer is accepted.

So yes, plan on it being cashed if you use this method. However, I've also found that most of the time if your offer is accepted they'll request a certified check made out to the correct place, not just title. So this can get the job done if you're in a pinch. Just cover your assets and make sure you have the amount in your account in case the offer is accepted and the check gets cashed.

Finally, you can use an alternative earnest money deposit date. This is similar to the promissory note, but it isn't as delayed. For the most part you can use an alternative earnest money date for up to 48 hours. You can request your agent put an alternative earnest money date in the contract. For example, "earnest money will be paid within 48 hours of acceptance." That way you can put in multiple offers and only have to worry about coming up with the earnest money if your offer is accepted. Also, with the 48 hour time frame after acceptance, you have 48 hours to find a buyer to put down the earnest money in your place. If it is a good enough deal, you'll have buyers competing for who gets the deal and who can put the earnest money down to secure the deal.

Proof of Funds

Proof of funds is a letter that is required just to make an offer. To make an offer through the MLS, you are usually required to have a proof of funds letter if you're paying cash, (or a prequalification letter if you are getting a loan to finance the deal). So it is a box you need to check. Do not delay; satisfy the need and get it done.

If you actually have cash or lines of credit (see funding options) then get a letter from your bank. If you do not have access to cash, it is okay if you're wholesaling because your buyers will be buying with cash. However, you'll still need the letter to place the offers. That being said, there are a handful of places you can go to get a proof of funds letter. See:

www.besttransactionfunding.com

www.insiderscash.com

www.linksourcemanagment.com.

Some of these sites require a membership fee, but by using them you will satisfy one of the requirements to make an offer.

Making Offers – Lots of Offers

Offer, offer, offer. It's as simple as that. You have to make a lot of offers to get a good deal under contract. This can be the most challenging part of being a wholesaler. It is very discouraging to look at a house, run the numbers, make an offer, and then get a "No" in response. After the first two, five, or even ten No's, a lot of people will just give up. I'm being brutally honest with you right now. You have to be resilient and power through. Expect the No's to come. This is a primary reason I like to spend as little time as possible on my offers. It makes it easier when the No's come.

So you may be asking how many offers you have to make. It is a common belief in the market that you have to make 25 offers to get one deal. That's a lot! Another way to look at this is to realize that every time you make an offer you only have a 4% chance of the offer being accepted. I know this may sound discouraging, but for me it actually helps me. If I know going in I only have a 4% chance of getting the deal, then I don't sweat the numbers or the "No" as much. It helps remind me to keep emotion out of it. Also if my Realtor tells me my offer will never be accepted, I can easily reply, "I realize I only have a 4% chance of getting this accepted, but this is what I have to offer to make the deal work."

Explaining your Creative Transaction

For an assignment, I submit the executed paperwork (both the purchase contract and assignment of contract) to the title company. I also include both the buyer's and seller's information so they can follow up with them. I explain I passed my rights to the contract on to the buyer for a fee. If the fee is being paid out at closing, I tell them to put me on the settlement statement (HUD statement) as a line item the buyer must pay. Then I ask if they'd like to mail, wire, or hand me the check after closing.

For a double close, I usually use the term "same day closing" or "simultaneous closing." Some title companies or attorneys do not know what a double close means. Once again I submit both executed contracts along with the seller's and buyer's information. I then tell them we'd like to buy and sell in the same day and use just one transferable title insurance policy. Most title policies have a time frame associated with them. Again these vary, but the time frame of a wholesale deal almost always falls within the policy's established time frame. Then I ask if I can use my buyer's money to close on the transaction with my seller (once again they cannot say yes unless you ask).

If I do need transactional funding, I'll call a transactional lender or hard money lender and get the ball rolling. The transactional lender can be the same company that provided the proof of funds letter or a referral from another investor. This lender will need the two contracts and the title company's information.

From there I see what questions they have. If they have additional questions and I don't know the answer I respond with, "My partner handles that side of the business. Let me check and get back to you." Ask your partner, ask another investor, ask your buyer, get the answer, and call them back.

The process of making offers is central to real estate investing. We've got more help to get you going!

Go to www.atimetoprofit.com/learn

"It is no use saying 'we are doing our best.' You have got to succeed in doing what is necessary."

Winston Churchill

Building Momentum –

Here are Some To-Do's:

- Find five to ten cash buyers

- Call, email, or send letters to these cash buyers

- Look at five homes and practice running numbers

- Make at least one offer

- Celebrate!

Chapter 4

Endless Possibilities: Lease Options

"If one advances confidently in the direction of his dreams, and endeavors to live the life which he has imagined, he will meet with a success unexpected in common hours."
Henry David Thoreau

I usually pride myself on following directions. That is truly a big part of my success. When I get a new appliance, I actually read the instruction manual and do what it says. Yep, I'm one of those. So I listen to what more experienced investors tell me to do and not do. Well, usually. There are exceptions. Wisdom says if you are going to embark on renovating a house, you should choose a light fixer-upper to begin with. "Light" means new flooring, paint, and maybe a few light fixtures.

One of my first fixers was anything but light. When I went to see it, there was water actively dripping in from the ceiling. The hardwood floors were literally soggy. It was like walking through a swamp. My advisor warned me against moving forward, but I had to learn this one the hard way. The renovation stretched from a planned four weeks to about four months. The costs nearly doubled from the expected budget. I had to get rid of one worn out nonperforming contractor and pay another to finally finish the monster.

Amazingly, I didn't lose money. I lost sleep but managed to find a family who could benefit from a lease-with-option-to-purchase. They loved this home, so we had a happy ending. However, the stress and loss of time could have been avoided. Listen to those who have gone before.

"I've got a woman's ability to stick to a job and get on with it when everyone else walks off and leaves it."
Margaret Thatcher

 I always wanted to get into the lease option side of the business. I love the idea of making money up front, having cash flow along the way, and a seeing a payoff at the end, as well. I mean three pieces of pie sound delicious anytime. However, it also seemed like a lot of work, not to mention the fact that I would have to manage the deal along the way. Additionally, almost all the seller financing lease option deals I came across wanted way too much down, so I figured I probably wouldn't be able to make the money up front. That being the case, it was always something I kept as an option in the back of my mind.

My father-in-law is one of my best bird dogs. He is a truly wonderful man and, best of all, he likes to talk to everyone. He had a co-worker who was offered his dream job. Currently they were working at a large medical campus in Denver, and this man was offered a job to manage the community recreation center at one of the popular mountain towns in Colorado. He couldn't pass up this opportunity, but it only left him two weeks in which to quit his current job, pack up, find a place to live, and make the move to the Rocky Mountains.

His first step was to call the Realtor who had helped him purchase the home a few years before. He had done a lot of work on it, including replacing the kitchen and bathroom, so he was hoping to get some good news. However, that didn't happen. The Realtor informed him that the house was worth about what he put into it, but to sell it quickly he'd have to sell it at a discount. Also, he would have to pay the Realtor's fee for selling the house out of the proceeds. In the best case scenario, selling the home was going to cost him a minimum of $5,000. He tried calling his lender to see if they would work with him in any way. They were not interested in being helpful, either.

In his frustration, he decided to just go into foreclosure. He thought it would tank his credit, but he'd be renting in the mountains anyways, so he'd just have to ride it out. One day, while feeling frustrated about his situation, he happened to vent to my father-in-law and asked if I would call him to discuss some options. My father-in-law called me with his co-worker's information, and I scheduled a time to meet with him between his packing and moving activities.

I saw the home, and it was in an okay neighborhood. Not the best, but not scary by any means. The home was a simple 900 square foot, two bedroom, and one bath house. On the plus side, it had two living spaces, a fenced yard, and a detached one car garage. We talked about what he needed to make on the house, what he owed, and what his payments were. It really came down to the fact that he was moving and didn't want or need the home. The bank was not interested in letting us assume his loan, so I mentioned the idea of a lease option. He said that as long as he didn't have to make the payments anymore he would be game.

I set up a three-year lease option with no money down. We would cover the payments (mortgage, taxes, and insurance). His only responsibility would be any repairs over $500 since he was still the owner. Even better, I didn't lock in a finalized sale price at the end of the three years. The only thing we put in the agreement was that if I chose to buy it I would pay only what was owed on the mortgage at that time. So I didn't put any money down, nor did I trap myself into a high price if I chose to close the deal. Additionally, we put a simple sublease clause in the contract so we could rent the property. I currently have the property rented for $307.50 more than the monthly payments. Finally, in my lease agreement, the tenant must maintain the property, pay all utilities, and cover costs for minor repairs.

No risk and no out of pocket costs, just $300/month profit plus the potential to make more money when I sell it if we choose to fulfill the lease terms. Not a bad way to make a lease option work for me.

"Imagination is the beginning of creation. You imagine what you desire, you will what you imagine, and at last, you create what you will."

George Bernard Shaw

Points to Ponder and Discuss:

Are you one of those people who think they have to do it all alone?

Are you able to accept help?

Think back to a time when you could have done something more efficiently or productively by seeking advice.

Is there something in your life right now, a decision or a situation, where you could benefit from an alternative perspective?

Lease Options

Lease options are a wonderful strategy for no money and no credit deals. These are different than wholesale deals because they have a few more moving parts. The great thing about lease options is the beauty of making money up front, making positive cash flow each month, and then making money again at the end when the option to buy is exercised.

This is also an ABC strategy where you are once again the savvy investor in the middle. The A player is still the motivated seller, but with a few variations. They may owe too much on the home to accept an aggressive cash offer. They may want to sell, but they may not be in dire straits yet, so the motivation is there without the urgency. They may be willing to hold the title longer and sell at a later date in order to not have to cover the payments during that time period and not have to be a landlord themselves. How do you find these motivated sellers? These motivated sellers can be found the same way as we described in the motivated seller section of the Wholesale chapter (Chapter 3), with a focus on the FSBO section.

The C buyer is not a cash buyer; they are a tenant buyer. A tenant buyer usually has had some sort of hardship. Often they are not that different than your motivated sellers, but they may be on the road to recovery. However, that's a slow road as we all learned in the recession that rocked our country during the last several years. Many times these tenant buyers have either lost their jobs during the recession, divorced, had health struggles, or been affected by a family member's death. This is a great opportunity for you to help another person get back on their feet. For many people who have had these struggles, the American dream of homeownership has become a thing of the past since their credit has been damaged or they've just started a new career. Create an opportunity for these individuals to keep that dream alive and make some money for yourself along the way.

Here are some ad descriptions for locating tenant buyers:

- Attention Renters!   Stop throwing $$$ away on rent. Learn how to RENT TO OWN a home and start building equity today!

- Attention Renters!   Build equity & rebuild your credit at the same time! Learn how easy it is to RENT TO OWN a home!

- Bankruptcy got you down?   Take the 1st step toward rebuilding your future today. Learn how easy it is to RENT TO OWN a home!

- Renters Don't Wait!   Learn how easy it is to RENT TO OWN. Get into a home today and start building equity!   Bankruptcy/Foreclosure OK

- Foreclosure got you down?   Learn how easy it is to RENT TO OWN and take the 1st step toward rebuilding your future!

- Fresh Start Program for Former Home owners!   Build equity & rebuild your credit at the same time. Learn how easy it is to RENT TO OWN a property! Bankruptcy/Foreclosure OK!

- Lost Your Home???   Begin again! Learn how easy it is to RENT TO OWN a property and start building equity & credit today!   Bankruptcy or Foreclosure OK!

Okay, we know who the players are. How do we make this happen? This is really all about negotiating terms that work for everyone involved. Have you ever heard the saying "I'll buy your house – Cash or terms." Well these are the terms they're talking about. The terms are longer than a quick close on a home. They are closer to the time frame of two to five years or more.

So let's start negotiating. We start with the motivated seller. This person may need to relocate and would like to sell their home, but they do not have the funds available to pay a Realtor their commission for selling the home. They may also be slightly upside down, meaning they owe more than the house is worth, so they cannot sell it without bringing money to the table. The best option for them may be to rent the property, but they may have no idea how to go about it or they may not want to be landlords. They may just want to have you take over their payments to relieve the stress a bit.

So what can you offer them? You offer to take the property off their hands for an extended period of time. Now in exchange for the right to take over their property, you may have to make a deposit or an option. An option is the right to potentially purchase the property in the future. The second step, in addition to the option, is the lease that sets the terms of the agreement including the payment amount and the time frame. Important things to consider are taxes and insurance. Make sure these will be covered by the payment you're making.

The seller will need to keep the house and these bills in their name while they are still the owner. To protect yourself, you can make sure these bills are sent to your mailing address. That way you can ensure they are paid. Also, another term you can write into the contract is a starting point. It may take you a bit of time to line up the right tenant buyer, so give yourself 30 to 90 days. Finally, when negotiating the option, you need to negotiate the final sales price for the end of the lease option term.

After you have an agreement in place with the seller, you need to find yourself the right tenant buyer. Marketing ideas are listed above. Hopefully, you've collected a list of potential tenant buyers from your marketing. If you do not have a tenant buyer, advertise the property on Craigslist as an available rent to own or lease option home. Once you get an interested tenant buyer, you start the negotiating process again. You'll negotiate the terms of the agreement the same as you did before.

First you start with the monthly lease: how much money you will charge each month and how long the lease term will be. If my lease with the seller is three to five years, then I'll try to make this lease two to three years. Make sure the rent amount covers all of your expenses with some cash flow left over for you. Next you will want to collect a non-refundable option fee from your tenant for the right to buy the home at the end of the lease option term.

Make sure the option fee is large enough to cover your option fee to the seller and a little bit of that up front profit that I was talking about. With the tenant, I want to make sure my option contract is a separate contract from the lease. Finally, in that option contract you want to once again make sure the end purchase price is higher than the one in your contract with the homeowner.

Lease Option Specifics

Motivated Seller

Once you have a motivated seller, you must:

- Negotiate the purchase price (for the future closing)

- Agree on the option payment you will make to the seller

- Set the time frame for the lease option

- Determine the monthly price you will pay to cover the seller's mortgage, insurance, and taxes

With the tenant buyer, you will:

- Negotiate the purchase price for the future closing (must be higher than the price you have negotiated with seller)

- Agree on the non-refundable option payment they will pay you (must be higher than your option to seller)

- Set the time frame for the lease option (must be less than your time frame with the seller)

- Determine the monthly payment they will pay you so that you can pay the buyer and have a monthly profit

Your Profit

Up Front:

Take the non-refundable option price that you negotiated with the buyer and subtract the option price you negotiated with the seller. This will be your up-front profit.

Along the Way:

Take the monthly payment your tenant buyer will pay you and subtract the monthly payment you will make to the seller. This will be your profit each month.

At the End:

Take the purchase price that you negotiated with the buyer for the future closing (less the cost of the option) and subtract the purchase price you negotiated with the seller (less the cost of the option). This will be your profit at the end of the deal.

Here's an example:

With your **motivated seller**, you negotiate a purchase price (for the future closing) of $110,000. You agree to an option payment of $2,000. The time frame for the lease option is set for 5 years, and the monthly price is determined to be $800 (to cover the seller's mortgage, insurance, and taxes on the property).

With your **tenant buyer**, you negotiate a purchase price for the future closing of $125,000. You agree to a nonrefundable option payment from them of $5,000. The time frame for the lease option is 3 years, and the monthly price is determined to be $1,100.

In this example, your profit will be as follows:

Up Front

Option price paid by buyer	$5,000
Option price you pay seller	- $2,000
Your profit up front	=**$3,000**

Along the Way

Monthly payment from tenant buyer	$ 1,100
Subtract the monthly payment to selle	-$ 800
Your profit each month	= $ 300

Your profit for 36 months ($300 x 36)   =**$10,800**

At the End

Payment from the buyer (less option) $120,000

Subtract payment to seller (less option <u>- $108,000</u>

Your profit at the end   = **$ 12,000**

Total Profit at the end of 3 years:

$3,000 + $10,800 + $12,000= **$ 25,800**

The scenario above is a description of a sandwich lease option, meaning you're the B in the middle of the A and C sandwich. There are several other options to explore when you're negotiating terms. Some loans allow you to assume the current loan, meaning you can just slip in and replace the current owner on the loan and deed. Another option, if you have good credit or access to money, is to buy the home outright and do a seller lease option to your tenant buyer with you as the owner. You can also do a buyer lease option with the seller where you have the right to sublease. This allows you to rent the property to someone else. This person does not have to be a tenant buyer but can be a traditional renter. Get creative and see what deals you can work out for yourself!

Profit here, there and everywhere. We don't want you to miss any of it!

Go to www.atimetoprofit.com/lear

"Think left and think right and think low and think high. Oh, the thinks you can think up if only you try."

Dr. Seuss

Building Momentum –

Here are Some To-Do's:

- Advertise on Craigslist for tenant buyers

- Call FSBO's and ask if they would be open to a rent-to-own solution

- Talk to a local real estate attorney to obtain the proper contracts for your state

Chapter 5

Expanding Your Strengths: Fix & Flip

"Success is a function of persistence and doggedness and the willingness to work hard for twenty minutes to make sense of something that most people would give up on after thirty seconds."

Malcolm Gladwell

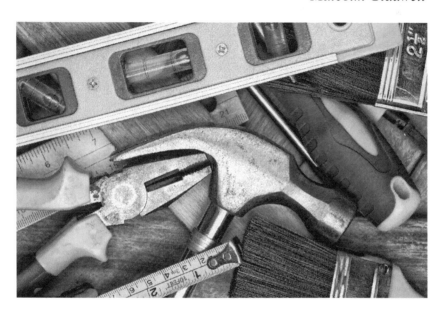

 You almost have to be as agile as a gymnast to pull off a successful flip. It's not the safest place to start. It is, however, how I started. For my first deal, I used money from our HELOC (home equity line of credit) and bought a house near my home for cash. That may sound risky, but I didn't feel like it was. I just plunged in. Ready, fire, aim. Some people go sky diving; I just invest in real estate!

I found a local contractor through a real estate agent I knew and trusted. Thankfully, this contractor knew a whole lot more than I did and headed up the whole project. I had little to say in what was done. Of course, that's not ideal. You really shouldn't do it that way. But it worked! I put the home on the market with a different Realtor I met at an Open House. I knew that this Realtor was hungry to sell and willing to learn the game with me. Incredibly, we had an offer that first weekend. The profit on that house was more than I had made in two or three years of teaching piano. Beginner's luck? I call it God's favor coupled with the willingness to walk on water and keep my eyes straight ahead.

"Ah, but a man's reach should exceed his grasp, or what's a heaven for?"

Robert Browning

So I had a couple of successful real estate investing years under my belt. I felt the urge to branch out and try a few more strategies – bigger strategies. Bigger strategies mean bigger rewards (money) but also bigger risk. So what's bigger than trying a fix-and-flip? Doing a fix-and-flip in a remote city.

The best way to start a long distance deal is to build a power team in that city. So we got to work. I gathered other wholesalers, construction partners, real estate agents, and an attorney. We spent a fair amount of time getting our team together and doing research before making offers. It took a while, but eventually we had a solid team in place.

I want to take a minute here to talk about our agreement with our construction partner. He was an investor we met through our research and networking in the Chicago market. We agreed that he would do the general contractor work for our project. The agreement stated that we would find, negotiate, and purchase the property. He would then pay for and manage all the rehab work. Then we would sell the property and split the profits. We felt that it was a good deal. Even though we had more money in the deal, the contractor had to invest money as well as time.

That being said, we negotiated a deal for a two flat property in south Chicago. The property was in solid shape structurally but needed a fair amount of work. Based on the sold comparable homes in the area, we felt the property would be worth roughly $200,000 after it was fixed up. We negotiated the property down to $75,000.

While our attorney was doing the title work to prepare for the closing, he discovered there was a demolition lien on the property. Our attorney did some further research and learned that this meant that the city would tear the property down if it sat vacant much longer. Additionally, the property had to be repaired and all repairs needed to be approved and inspected by the city. These were all things we were planning on doing anyway.

However, I know an opportunity when I see one. The fact that the demolition lien showed up meant that the bank selling the property was in a tight position. Number one, they should have disclosed that to us. Number two, anyone who wanted to purchase the property but needed to have financing to do so would not be able to buy it. So why not renegotiate? This was the perfect opportunity to ask for a lower purchase price. And that's what I did.

I went back to the bank and told them about the demolition lien. They claimed to have no knowledge of it. I explained, in extreme examples, worst case scenarios, what needed to be done to remove the lien. I also stated we would be happy to purchase the property, but due to this circumstance we needed a lower price, specifically $45,000 instead of $75,000. The bank said they couldn't go that low, but to cover their costs they could give us the property for $47,500. Perfect. Once again I was able to take another $27,500 off the price of the property just by asking.

From there we got to work. What should have only taken two to three months turned into a rehab nightmare. We ran into endless problems with the city as we tried to get plans approved and inspections done. It was incredible getting councilmen and aldermen to sign off and approve our plans. We were dealing with "licensed" contractors only to find out they were using someone else's license, forcing us to redo the work. Finally, it was a 3-1/2 month process of closing the property after we had it fixed up. There were issues with the appraiser; in fact, we ended up having three different ones. And, of course, we had issues with the underwriting of the loan.

Finally, after 15 long months, we closed the deal. It was a good thing I still knew how to wholesale and was able to do several more deals while we waited for this deal to close. When it was all said and done, after taxes, insurance, utilities, holding costs, and closing costs, we made $25,000 and so did our construction partner. Again, $25,000 is a great profit, but I felt like I truly earned it at the end of those 15 months. Even more than the money, I learned a ton about rehabs, contractors, and city government. It was a long stressful deal, but I'm a better investor because of it.

"Edison failed 10,000 times before he made the electric light. Do not be discouraged if you fail a few times."
Napoleon Hill

Points to Ponder and Discuss:

What are your greatest strengths?

How have these propelled you forward in life?

What are your weaknesses?

How can you use someone else's expertise in these areas?

Can you develop a life strategy to continue to grow your strengths and utilize other people's strengths to compensate for your weaknesses?

Think back on your life experiences. What has occurred to prepare you for the next chapter of your life?

What do you enjoy?

What makes you feel happy and fulfilled?

How can you couple this with your strengths and experiences to propel you through an open door?

Do you see the door?

 Maybe I relish a good flip because my dad was a carpenter, and I learned to love the smell of sawdust! You find a house that looks horrible – the kind where most people don't make it past the front door. The poor baby has been neglected, even abused, maybe even stinks. You may have to breathe through your shirt collar. Ah! Perfectly wonderful. Mismatched doors, holes in drywall, cotton candy pink walls decorated artistically with graffiti. Smurf blue bathtubs, avocado appliances and burnt orange shag carpet. Beautiful in every way. Potential is what you are looking at. Potential the ordinary sort of gal or guy just doesn't see.

There is one note of strong caution I must provide before we enter into the discussion of flipping houses. This is risky. There's no way around that fact. Lots of stuff can go wrong. You can lose a lot of money. I recommend you get your feet wet in the world of wholesaling and lease options and other safer playgrounds before you flip. Do as I say, not as I do. I started my real estate investment career with a sweet flip.

I'll tell you the story. I found a local agent to work with right here in my backyard of Seattle. Starting in your own backyard is another recommendation I have for you, and hey, I actually followed this one. We had been putting in offers, lots and lots of offers. There was one house in particular I liked. The neighborhood was just right for investing. It was a safe entry-level neighborhood. The house had a view of the hillside and was on a quiet dead end street. At the end of this street was a park with walking trails and around the block was the elementary school in a highly rated school district. Who wouldn't want to live there?

That's point number one of this story. You have to select a house to flip in a neighborhood where lots of folks would like to live. It's just common sense. Busy streets, commercial areas, behind freeways – these are not good choices. I had put an offer on this house two times. Both times my offer was rejected and the bank who owned the property accepted another offer. Both times the accepted offer fell through. Serves them right! I had put in a third offer on this same house. I'd practically forgotten I even had the offer out there and certainly was not expecting it to get accepted.

Meanwhile, I was attending an auction and bought a house there. I called my agent to let him know he was about to make a few bucks on my auction purchase. I could hardly get the words out before he burst in and told me that the bank accepted my offer!

Point number two of the story – don't give up, keep submitting the offers. Golly, gee, good news, but how am I going to fund two deals? I figured it out by getting a traditional mortgage on my auction house and using funds from our Home Equity Line of Credit for the other.

Next I needed a contractor. I was able to get several good referrals (always the best way to go), got bids, and we were off to the races. Points number three and four of the story: find your contractors through reliable referrals and get multiple bids. We had that house renovated and sold in six weeks, including Christmas week. The profit from this deal went a long way toward paying college tuition.

I love the positive impact that buying, renovating, and reselling a house has. Let's take a look. Number one, you are buying a house, so your real estate agent makes money. That's good. Number two, you are renovating the house, so your contractor makes money. That's good. Number three, you are turning an ugly house into a beautiful home for a family. That's good. Number four. You make a pile of money when you sell the house. That's very, very good. Number five, because of the new life you brought to this home, the whole neighborhood is improved. That's good. Number six. You do this over and over, and one house at a time America is restored. That's great. See what I mean? Flipping is wonderful.

Let's examine the steps of a buy, fix, and resell which is what I call flipping. The first thing you have to do is find the house. You can find houses in two ways. One is working with a real estate agent for properties listed on the MLS. The second way is using your own marketing to dig up deals that are not listed. It's exactly what you would do if you were planning to wholesale, so I'll let you refer to that chapter for the details.

There is one difference when I'm planning to keep the deal myself and flip it versus wholesale it. I may go after new listings if the numbers work. Usually for wholesaling you are looking for houses that have been on the market longer than usual or have had a price reduction. It's all about numbers; you cannot get emotionally involved. This took me awhile to learn. It's so easy to get excited about the potential you see and be tempted to pay too much. You can't do that or you are reducing your profit before you even begin. It also doesn't matter if you actually like the house. What matters is that a lot of other people would like the house, so don't let your personal preferences influence you.

People like vanilla. I like vanilla, too, but usually when I go out for ice cream, I'll order something like Jamaican Almond Fudge or Spumoni. So I struggle picking out vanilla houses. I like creative, contemporary floor plans, but that's like Spumoni – I need vanilla for my investment houses. I have trained myself now. I look for vanilla, maybe chocolate, but that's it! You want to buy houses that suit the largest segment of the population.

This is also the same as the houses you select for wholesaling. You want three or four bedroom homes with two baths (or the ability to add that second bath). You want decent but modest neighborhoods. You don't want a house that is already pretty. The way you create your profit is by adding value. However, you also don't want a house that is a complete disaster, about to fall in on itself (I've done that too, but that's another story). Those houses take too much time and money to renovate. You could do two or three moderate renovations and make two or three piles of money in the same time. Generally, you buy in nice first-time-homebuyer neighborhoods because this is where there is the highest number of potential homeowners. If you invest in more expensive areas, you are limited by the number of people who can afford to live there.

You make offers. When I am looking at investment properties, there are only three reasons I will not make an offer. Number one, the floor plan is weird – you know, Jamaican Almond Fudge-like. Not enough people will like it. This could be because of too many additions or because the architect had a wild imagination. Number two, the location is terrible. Number three, the cost of purchase and renovation would be higher than the price for which the home could be resold. Hence, you make many, many offers. You expect and accept No's and stick to your numbers. This is similar to wholesaling, once again, so review the Running the Numbers section in Chapter 3. The only difference is you don't have to deduct the wholesaler's profit because now you are the cash buyer.

Once you have a property under contract (i.e. you and the seller have agreed upon the price and terms), you need to carefully inspect the home. You don't necessarily have to pay for a property inspection because your contractors will do this for free in hopes of getting the job. Get bids during your inspection period. Then you know how much the renovation is really going to cost.

Once you have inspected the home with either a licensed inspector or your contractor and are comfortable with the project, close on the house. Now, *once you are experienced* and *have a team in place you can trust*, you may make your offers without a property inspection contingency. Your team will check out the house for you once you are negotiating with the seller. Your offer is stronger without contingencies, but be careful if you do this!

Congratulations. You now own an investment property, but it still looks like garbage. This is where the real fun begins. I want you to use a cookbook approach and create a recipe for renovating houses. I wish I had understood this approach when I did my first few flips. Man, I wasted so much time, and you know, time is money. I would personally run from Home Depot to Lowe's, and back to Home Depot to select just the right light fixture. Wait, better see what's available at Seattle Lighting. Nope, liked the one at Home Depot better.

This is not going to be your home! You just need vanilla, remember? Get yourself a latte (vanilla maybe) and go spend a couple of hours in your local home improvement store. List the items you want to use in all of your renovations by SKU number. Pick out back-up items as well and note those SKU numbers. Also, note the price and installation costs if available. Give this list to your contractors. They will use it to build their bids and buy the materials. You never have to think about it again. What? You think it will be boring if all your renovations look the same? Vanilla. Plain vanilla sells.

I prefer to pay for the materials directly. I have my contractors estimate the cost of material and labor separately. I have a credit account at the home improvement store, and my contractors are authorized to make purchases on this account. I can see everything they purchase, know it's for my project, and material costs cannot be marked up.

You want to create a neutral, new, and modern palette without spending a fortune doing it. Typically, here is what will need to be done. On the outside, if the roof will not pass a five-year certification, you will replace it. If the windows are ancient and all the neighbors are replacing them, you will need new windows. How's the exterior paint? Old or ugly? Repaint. Curb appeal is everything. Change the color of the front door and add or remove shutters. Clean up the yard, trim the shrubs, and add a touch of color, but don't get carried away.

Inside, new interior paint in a vanilla-like color (read beige). Use white trim or leave the wood natural. Add new floors everywhere – new carpet if that's what's popular in your area or new vinyl/tile/laminate. Again, do whatever is the norm in your area. If there is hardwood hiding under that stinky carpet, refinish it. Everyone loves hardwood. You want all new light fixtures, door knobs and hinges in brushed nickel. In the kitchen, a new stainless set of appliances, new counters, sink and faucet, and oftentimes new cabinets. In the bathrooms, you usually want a new vanity, sink, and faucet, and maybe a new toilet. If the tub is white, bone, or beige, just get it shiny clean. If it's blue, green, gold or pink, get it resurfaced. Interior doors need to match. You may have to replace all of those.

Don't forget the little things, like towel racks, window blinds, and new electrical outlets and plates. You want this to look like a brand new house. Then there are the major mechanicals. The HVAC, hot water tank and electrical panel must be up to date and functional. Aren't you glad you are using a general contractor and you created a recipe?

You ought to be able to finish a renovation in two to six weeks. It's going to depend on how finely tuned your team is and how big the job is. You will want to require a two to three- man team because one guy alone takes forever, and what happens if he gets sick or disappears on you? Well, I could answer that question with another story, but I'll resist. Trust me. Use a two to three-man team.

Here's another cautionary note. One thing is almost certain: Something is going to go wrong in the renovation process. Something expensive is going to be found that no one could see until the process began. Therefore, do two things. Figure a buffer in your numbers and plan for a bigger profit than will satisfy you. Frankly, I usual run my numbers with a planned profit of double what would satisfy me. That way, I'm seldom disappointed.

Once the house is renovated and perfectly clean, you may want to have it professionally staged. I do not always do this, but it is often worth it. Staged houses sell faster. People have embarrassingly little imagination. I like to hang an American flag outside as well. What will be your trademark detail?

List your home with an agent who is prominent and successful in the area. Certain agents seem to own neighborhoods, and there's usually a good reason for that. People trust them because they do their job well. You need an agent who is aggressive in marketing. Ask them what they would do to get your house sold. Interview a few agents, and let them know you are considering your options. Once you have a relationship established, you will probably use the same agent over and over again. It's great if the agent you bought the house from is the same agent who lists it. He's going to make two commissions on one house! This is incentive to work really hard to find you more deals.

A house overpriced by five percent won't sell. Don't be greedy. Have your agent run a comparable market analysis (CMA) to determine the fair market value of the house, and then price it a little lower. Yes, you heard me – lower it. Pigs get fat. Hogs get slaughtered. Your goal is to sell the house fast and move on to your next deal. Price the house to sell in 30 days or less. You don't want to have to reduce the price. Once you do, the house is suspect. People wonder what is wrong, and you are likely to get low offers. I've got another story about pricing a home too high, in fact several, but I'll resist again. Price it right the first time, and sell it fast.

Once you sell the house, please go celebrate! There is nothing like marking our successes to keep us going. If you just pay off your bills and reinvest, you won't be as satisfied as if you take even a little teeny bit of that profit and do something special. Take yourself and a friend to dinner, take a mini-vacation, or buy something for yourself that you wouldn't ordinarily buy.

Here I'll tell a little story. After flipping a house once, I was shopping with a friend. That's always a good idea for us ladies, because we encourage each other to buy. There was a Jo Malone perfume I had been drooling over for months. You know, I was stopping to smell and apply it every time I went shopping. It was expensive. I wouldn't dare buy it, but I did! I bought it, and I love it to this day. Every time I apply the sweet scent of While Lilacs and Rhubarb, I smell not only springtime but success. It helps me to keep pushing ahead.

Last but not least, I encourage you to give back. Set aside a portion of your profits and donate to your church or a charity, or help a family in need. That is true success.

 Thought of a renovation make you shaky? Let me give you some assurance.

Go to www.atimetoprofit.com/learn

Building Momentum –

Here are Some To-Do's:

- Visit Lowe's or your local home improvement store

- Make a list of renovation materials

- Identify one or two potential flip properties

- Get three bids from contractors

- Run the numbers, include:

    - Holding costs (taxes, insurance, utilities, etc.)
    - Closing costs
    - Realtor fees

Chapter 6

Uncover True Wealth and Prosperity: Buy and Hold

"Being rich is having money; being wealthy is having time."
Margaret Bonnano

I had gotten into the swing of things. That's not to say that I still wasn't full of anxiety and losing sleep the night before a closing or locking up a deal or the night after putting in a lot of offers. Yes, I have a tendency to lose sleep when I cannot control everything. However, I didn't have to ask for help nor did I really need to have anyone explain to me how a deal works. We were making money and paying down some debt and with that reducing our stress levels. Even better, we were taking control of our lives for the future.

I had the feeling that we were running out of properties, though. I was getting listings from my agents, but there weren't a lot of new properties on the lists each week. If I wanted to do more and go faster, we had to branch out further. So I dove into the Greater Denver Metro Area, but I didn't stop there. I decided I couldn't just focus on single family homes. In addition to single family homes, Denver is full of a many styles of condos, attached units and multifamily living units. So I went to work again.

I managed to get a four-plex locked up six miles down the street from the State Capitol. I was pretty excited and surprised by the price that was accepted. Even though it needed a fair amount of work, it was a great price. After talking to some buyers, though, I learned that the neighborhood wasn't the best and most people were not interested in buying due to the area. That's when I understood why they accepted my price! A great lesson learned in branching out. Just because I knew the strategies didn't mean that when I expanded I would be successful using them. You need to know the areas and you need to know what your buyers want, especially when you are wholesaling.

The other issue I ran into was that all my buyers in Denver wanted to do fix and flips, not rentals. Home prices in Denver are high which makes it harder, even with good rents, to get a good return on investment. A multifamily is not ideal since they cannot

101

sell it to a "retail buyer" once it is fixed up. That being the case, I had to dig in once again and expand my buyers list. I ran a lot of ads and talked to everyone I could, especially at REI clubs. I even offered to team up and split the profit with anyone who had a buyer.

In the long run, that's how I was able to get the deal done on the four-plex. There was another investor in the area who found a great landlord buyer for us. I had the property locked up at $145,000 and double closed it for $155,000. I was able to make $5,000 for us and $5,000 for the investor who brought the buyer. Once again, we made some cash, and all parties involved were happy with the result.

"Develop success from failure. Discouragement and failure are two of the surest stepping stones to success."

Dale Carnegie

 My number one focus in real estate is growing our net worth through rental properties. Retirement pension plans are a thing of the past. Social security is now in question for the future. If we want to have a retirement, passive income is the way for us. I have focused on buying a minimum of eight rental properties a year and will continue to do so until I reach a position where the cash flow each month will support the lifestyle we want to live.

I utilize a method of buying properties with cash (either our own or private money) and then fixing up the properties so they are in rent-ready condition. Once I have rented out a property, I approach a small local bank for a "cash out refinance." I do not always get all my money out, but I get most of the money back. Once refinanced, I'm in a position to do it all over again.

Here is the last deal that I did with a "cash out refinance." I purchased a property in Minneapolis, Minnesota for $35,000. The property needed a fair amount of work to get cleaned up. In total I spent $31,000. I then turned the property over to property management to secure a tenant. The rent received each month is $1,200, with the tenant paying all the utilities. Monthly expenses are as follows:

$ 91.00 Taxes
$ 84.50 Insurance
$ 80.00 Property Management
$ 50.00 Vacancy (1/2 month rent / 12 months)
$120.00 Reserves (10% rent)
$425.50 Total monthly expenses

Here is a breakdown of our cash flow each month:

Rent $1,200.00

Minus Expenses $ 425.50

Monthly Cash Flow $ 774.50 before cash out refinance

My total investment in the property, including purchase, repairs, and closing costs, was approximately $70,000. The property appraised for $124,000 and our bank was willing to loan us up to 75% of that value. I was able to take out a total of $93,000 on this property, which is $23,000 above what we put into the deal. Additionally, since this was a refinance and we took equity out, we are not taxed on that $23,000 because it is not earned income. (Note: Be sure to consult with a tax accountant.) In my opinion, that is better than a rehab where I'll be taxed on short-term capital gains.

The monthly mortgage payment on this property is $698.65. This cuts our monthly cash flow to $75.85 per month ($774.50 - $698.65). Now I know I cannot retire on that cash flow alone. This was a decision I made to free up more cash (the additional $23,000) to purchase future properties to continue to grow our net worth. This allows me to purchase more properties while the economy is still slow in order to reach our financial goals. The best news is that our tenants are paying off each property, helping us increase our cash flow and fund our future life.

Points to Ponder and Discuss

Think about what it would take in your life for you to feel secure.

What are the financial factors?

The health factors?

The social factors?

The spiritual factors?

How do you define wealth and prosperity?

Think back to a time in your life when you didn't walk through a door because you didn't feel secure about it.

How would your life be different today if you had taken that step?

What steps can you take NOW to move your life in the direction you desire?

Buy and Hold

 Passive income is the basis of wealth building. There is nothing like going to the mailbox the first week of the month and pulling out a handful of checks. Happy trip to the bank, month after month! Of course, you could get these auto-deposited, but I like holding them in my hand and patting myself on the back. Way to go! You are getting paid over and over again for a little bit of work that you did one time.

There are so many great reasons to hold real estate. Traditional investors believe in diversifying their portfolio, keeping some in stocks, some in 401(k)s, and some in real estate. Of course, there are those who take exception to that approach and advise you put it all in real estate where you are in control! I'm not going to debate that, but rather just tell you to get in the game and own some rentals. You won't be sorry if you do it the right way.

What is the right way? First of all, hold properties in areas where you will receive an excellent return on your money, and be sure you have at least a bit of equity in them from the start. What do I mean? Well, if I were going to hold a property in Vancouver, BC, I would have to spend probably a minimum of $300,000. If I were getting a 5% return, that would be considered good. Ugh! If I were to hold a property in Seattle, I'd have to spend around $200,000, and a return of 9-10% would be considered good. Better. If I were to hold a property in areas like the suburbs of Detroit, Cleveland, Kansas City, Memphis, or Montgomery, I would spend $20,000 to $75,000 and get a return of 15% or more!

Now that makes good financial sense to me. How about you? There are investors who just cannot get comfortable holding properties they cannot personally drive to see. That's a pretty limiting problem. The good news for you is that those are the guys you wholesale to. You are going to be a level-headed business person and make your decisions based on numbers.

Let's explore the numbers you need to consider when you are ready to hold a property. The objective here is quite different than what it would be if you were going to flip a house. However, it is similar to how you would run your numbers if you were going to wholesale to a landlord, so pay extra attention here. Again, I suggest never buying a property with no equity in it. In other words, you are an investor, so you want to buy houses at a price lower than retail. However, with rentals, that is secondary. The primary number you are looking for is your return.

Now, I am not an accountant. (I have an excellent accountant on my team, just like I have great real estate agents, contractors, and property managers.) So I'm going to explain this in a non-accountant way. The terms Return on Investment (ROI), Capitalization (CAP) Rate, and Cash on Cash Return (COCR) are used rather loosely to mean the same thing.

Again, my accountant could tell you the differences, but it doesn't matter for this discussion. Simply, it is the percent your money earns. What is a good number here? Well, if you have any money in the bank, you are probably earning less than 1%. If it's in a CD, it is earning you maybe 2 or 3%. Traditional IRA's and 401(k)'s earn 10% or more when they are thriving, but they can sink back down to 2% or less as the markets fluctuate. Stocks? Now that's a gamble in my opinion. You can make a bundle and lose it the next day, just like at the poker table, but you don't have to wear sunglasses.

Currently, I am still able to find deals with a 15+% return. As the housing market continues to rebound, that's going to become harder to do. So start now! Here is how you calculate the return on your investment.

Let's say the property you are looking at will rent for $1,000 a month. There are monthly expenses that must be considered:

insurance, taxes, property management fees, and a reserve for maintenance and vacancies.

Consider this: $1,000 rent
Minus $65 insurance
              $150 taxes
              $100 property management fees
              $75 cash reserve
              $610 net monthly

For this discussion, we are not considering a mortgage payment.

Multiply the net monthly cash flow by 12 and you get what is called Net Operating Income (NOI).

$610 x 12 months = $7,320

Next we take the amount paid for the home plus the cost of renovations. This figure is commonly referred to as the "all in" amount.

Let's say you pay $50,000 for the house and spend $20,000 in renovations. You are "all in" for $70,000.

One more calculation and we are there. Divide the NOI by your "all in" number.

$7,320/$70,000 = 10.4%

That is your ROI, and 10% is pretty good by anyone's standards. But you can do even better.

If you aren't happy with this ROI, you have to pay less, keep your renovation costs down, reduce your monthly expenses, or increase your rent. However, do not assume you can get more than the going rate for rent. You want your tenants happy and not looking to move to a cheaper place as soon as their lease expires.

In a nutshell, those are the numbers you will be running for properties you hold.

Let's talk about property management. Please remember you are the investor. Not the contractor, not the accountant, not the attorney, and NOT the property manager. I am a huge proponent of using professional property management companies now, but when I first started in this business, I didn't even know they existed.

I first learned about property management services when I talked to a woman sitting next to me at my local real estate investment club meeting. She said that she was a property manager. What did that mean? She explained what she did. What would it cost me? She said that I would pay one month's rent for her to find a tenant and 10% of the rent for her to manage the property. What? I gasped. You'll do all that for 10%? Fantastic! I don't have to answer the phone. Leaking toilets – not my problem! Love it. Once you have several properties, you may be able to negotiate these standard rates even lower. Again, a rule to remember in real estate: everything is negotiable!

How do you select properties to hold? There are a lot of philosophies on that. Here is mine: I like to hold properties in safe neighborhoods. Usually this is in what I call the first ring suburbs of a major city. I pick neighborhoods where most of the homes are owner occupied; I don't choose neighborhoods that are primarily rentals. I like to see pride in home ownership – cut lawns, trimmed bushes, shoveled snow, and pumpkins on the front steps in the fall.

When I rent in these neighborhoods, I can usually get a great tenant who takes care of the property. Sometimes this can even turn into a rent-to-own situation. The other reason I pick my holds in these kinds of neighborhoods is because I can generally get more equity, and the values tend to increase more quickly than in neighborhoods full of rentals. Ask yourself, "Would I live here?" For me, if the answer is "no," I don't buy it.

Renovations for a property that is going to be a rental are different than for properties you are going to flip. You still want to make a nice home, but you don't have to do as much. If it isn't going to increase the rent, attract a better quality tenant, or cause the house to rent more readily and the tenant to stay longer, don't do it.

I'll give you some examples. If the roof has a few years left in it, you aren't going to replace it. If the windows are functional but old, you aren't going to replace them. If the kitchen cabinets are serviceable, you are likely to clean or paint them and put on new hardware, but not replace them. See where I'm going here? I do add little zing items like a tile backsplash or a rainfall shower head. Makes the house fly off the market!

You've selected a good neighborhood, purchased a property, and had it renovated to a level that will attract a quality tenant. In the meantime, you have been calling property management companies. I suggest you get referrals for these from your real estate investment club. You want your property management company to begin advertising right away. Get a tenant in there right after the renovations are done and start collecting checks from your mailbox. Congratulations! You've taken a big step to building wealth.

Here's the icing on the cake. I mean, who wants cake without icing? You call all the small community banks, credit unions, and mortgage companies in the area of your rental. You are looking for a bank that will allow you to do a "no season" refinance. "No season" means that you do not have to own the property for any certain period of time before you can refinance it.

You start by asking the banks if they have portfolio or in-house loans. Yes? Good. I like to buy homes for cash and then refinance them as soon as I finish the renovations. Will you do that? Yes. Great. What percent loan to value will you allow? 75-80%? Wonderful. Are these loans reported to the credit bureau? (Preferably, you don't want these refinances showing up on your credit record) No. Fantastic. What is your aggregate? (The most a bank will loan any one individual.) Up to $1 billion. Love it. (Well, $200,000 isn't a bad start either.) Now you pull out all the cash you have in the property, sometimes even more, and go buy yourself another rental. This is the crème de la crème.

 ROI – my oh my – Seeing that calculation explained in a video certainly couldn't hurt!

Go to www.atimetoprofit.com/learn

"Wherever you see a successful business, someone once made a courageous decision."

Peter Drucker

Building Momentum –

Here are Some To-Do's:

- Interview three property management companies

- Practice running ROI on two potential rentals

- Call at least 20 local banks and interview them about "no season" refinance

Chapter 7

Compound Your Success: Turnkey Real Estate and Full Service Wholesaling

"It's hard to be a diamond in a rhinestone world."
Dolly Parton

 My very first deal was a bird dog deal. Over the years I've heard this strategy is just for beginners and that more experienced investors don't do it. I was thinking about that concept and decided that line of thinking was crazy. That initial bird dog deal made me $4,400, and it was one of the easiest deals I've ever done. So if I made good money with less stress, less time, less effort, and helped people in the process, then why wouldn't I want to do more of these deals?

I talked to an investor partner in Minnesota I had worked with on several rental deals. His business model is providing full-service investments. The investor only has to provide the cash. This partner then purchases the house, renovates it, puts a tenant in place, and hires property management. I knew people who would like that model, so we discussed the idea of him paying referral fees for buyer leads. He said he'd be happy to do that, as he always has deals coming in and he was hoping to expand into a couple other markets. We went back and forth on the fee, and he said he'd be happy to split the profits. How great is that? I do half the work – less than half really – and I get half the profits. Sounds great to me! I told him it was a deal, and I'd get to work on my end.

I started talking up my returns and cash flow on my out-of-state rental properties. These kinds of returns are just not possible in the Denver market due to our high home prices. It really got people's attention. I'd usually have dinner with them and explain the process of the investments, set the expectations that this is a long-term hold strategy but also introduce them to banks in the market so they could cash out for another investment. From there I would send out introduction emails to my team members in Minnesota.

I was able to do six deals this way last year by just referring people and made over $12,000 for simply offering an opportunity and making an introduction. I've decided that if this strategy is just for beginners, I'm content to be a beginner forever! It's nice to know that even after a ton of different real estate experiences, I can still come full circle back to where I started in a totally different economic time and make money with the same strategy as before. Life is good!

"Simplicity is the ultimate sophistication."
Leonardo Da Vinci

 When the time came that I started traveling to teach real estate investment, I was gone from home a lot. It was quite the change from stay-at-home mom, and I just loved it. There was a guy in my local real estate investment club who had asked to go to coffee with me several times. I was too busy. (Did I think I was too important?) I realized this was a horrible attitude. Hadn't several experienced investors from my club made time to meet with me when I was new to the game? Yes. So I agreed to a coffee at Starbucks (since I'm in Seattle, Starbucks is on every corner). We met. He bought my coffee. We shared. I made suggestions. I referred him to a remote turnkey investor I knew who I thought might provide him with the kind of investment he wanted. An hour went by. Another half hour went by. Time spent: 110 minutes including travel. A month went by. My husband walked in with the mail and an open envelope in his hand. "What's this?" Clearly, it was a $1,000 check, written to yours truly. A bird dog fee for the referral!

$1,000/110 minutes = $9/minute = $545/hour

Yes, a simple referral is an easy wholesale strategy. Don't ignore simple. That was the most rewarding cup of coffee I've ever had!

"The fact that I can plant a seed and it becomes a flower, share a bit of knowledge and it becomes another's, smile at someone and receive a smile in return, are to me continual spiritual exercises."

Leo Buscaglia

Points to Ponder and Discuss:

Close your eyes.

Picture your life as you want it to be twelve months from now.

What does it look like?

How do you feel?

What have you achieved?

What are you doing that helps those around you to improve their lives?

Open your eyes and immediately write down five action steps. Don't over-think it.

These strategies are really the concierge business of real estate. These are next level strategies that can bring in great consistent cash for you and your business. Turnkey real estate is the selling of properties that are completely ready to go. "Ready to go" means they have been rehabbed, rented, and have property management in place. Full service is similar, but instead of doing the repair, renting and management up front, or even the fix-and-flip efforts, it is a service that is offered as part of the deal. Basically, a full service wholesaler lines up everything needed to find, renovate, manage, and possibly even finance the property. The wholesaler does not do the actual work, but they manage a team that provides these services. Thus you provide full service and gain additional profit.

Turnkey Real Estate

Turnkey real estate is a business that usually requires a fair amount of cash to get up and running. The principles of wholesaling come in handy when it comes to turnkey real estate deals. First you have to get a great deal. If you don't have a great deal, it is hard to add value. In addition to having a great deal, you'll need a team to get the property all ready to go. The initial team members you'll need will be those who help you find the great deal: your Realtor, another wholesaler, bird dogs, or even your own marketing. From there you'll need contractors and property management people to take that great deal and make it profitable. You'll need a good contractor you can depend on to consistently transform your property to a livable and desirable condition. Also have a property manager you can count on to consistently find good and qualified tenants for the properties. In addition to these main players, having an insurance agent who offers rental hazard insurance policies for the homes is a bonus.

Think of turnkey as an all-encompassing service that requires the owners to do nothing other than close on the property. Wow, well that sure sounds like a lot of work for you. Why would you be interested in this? First, you can sell the home closer to retail value as it is move-in ready. The better shape the property is in and the fact that the property is already creating income all adds value to the property. Additionally, you'll have access to more buyers. There are a lot of individuals out there who have cash and are looking for better investments for their money. Many people are interested in real estate for investing purposes, but they do not have the time or the education to make a proper investment. This is exactly where you come in and make a nice profit. Again, be aware this does require some upfront money, yours or other creative options – see the funding chapter, so you can fund the purchase, repair and hold while it gets rent ready.

Full Service Wholesaling

Full service wholesaling does not require money up front but still requires a solid team to perform the services you offer. Full service is a great direction to branch into after you've done a few wholesale deals. You've mastered finding good deals, now you need to start building up your team. These will be the same team members listed above in the turnkey section, but also gives you the option to offer fix and flip services. Start networking and build a team you can count on.

Okay, now you've got a team. How do you make this work? You start the same way you would if you were wholesaling. Find some potential buyers. Just like in turnkey, they do not need to already be fix and flip or landlord buyers. They just need to be people with cash or with access to cash who are willing to make an investment backed by real estate. Once you have some potential buyers on board, go out and find a great deal for either a fix and flip or a rental. Get a bid from your contractor on the costs to get it renovated and resold or rented. Confirm the resale price with your Realtor or the rental value with your property manager.

Once you have a full picture of what it is worth, the cost of the repairs, and the profit for the resell or the monthly cash flow for a rental, you have something to present to potential buyers. This is a great opportunity for you to make money during many parts of the process (kind of like lease options). First you wholesale the property for a profit. Second you manage the rehab for the buyer, which will give you a bit of a profit as well. Lastly, you can get a referral fee from the other team members when they rent or sell the property because you helped them make money by bringing in a new client. Now just rinse and repeat!

Help Them Buy More

Now that you've got a turnkey or full service real estate business up and running, you can help your buyers do more deals, and in turn you can make more money. If you add a small local bank willing to do cash out refinances, you really can rinse and repeat. Helping a landlord investor get their money out of a rental property can leverage their buying power. Yes, that will decrease their monthly cash flow, but it will increase their net worth and the ability to do more deals. That equates to more money for them in the long run and more money for you right now.

 Not so sure how to find a bank to do these no-season refis – or even quite what there are? We've got the answers.

Go to www.atimetoprofit.com/learn

Building Momentum –

Here are Some To-Do's:

Build a Full Team

- Contractors

- Property Management

- Insurance

- Title Company

- Attorney

- Local Banks for refinancing

Chapter 8

Expanding Your Resources:
Funding Your Deals

"If you are not going to put money in real estate, where else?"

Tamir Sapin

 To those of you in my age category (the category where you are seriously thinking about retirement funds), listen up. *Holding homes for passive income is your goal.* Shelter is a basic human need. It will always be true that people need to have a roof overhead. Your job is to buy up as many roofs as possible, and luckily, those roofs are always attached to homes.

My goal is to own enough homes so that we have enough passive income to do nothing but what we choose to do. That doesn't necessarily mean not working. I'm not sure we were created to retire. We are happiest when we are productive and helping those in our lives. I just don't want to be a slave to a job, especially one that has a boss connected to it.

One fantastic way to fund homes is with a self-directed IRA. You can take funds from an existing IRA and transfer them to a self-directed IRA with no tax penalty. I am not an accountant or attorney, so you must seek professional advice to do this correctly.

Like many of you, my husband and I took a substantial hit on our retirement accounts during one of the roller coaster dips the stock market likes to take. Here's our solution. We self-directed a healthy portion of the funds remaining and bought a bunch of homes. These houses provide an excellent, stable return on our investment. They don't experience the ups and downs of the market. Rent stays the same or goes up. We buy houses in stable neighborhoods where vacancy is seldom an issue.

Now I am not a landlord, er, landlady! The last thing I want is a call about the sink leaking. I use property management companies. So my only involvement in these rentals is watching the retirement account grow. When enough cash accumulates, I find another nice rental and buy it. The self-directed IRA account has babies! Once you hit 59½ years old, you can withdraw funds with no tax penalty. Amazingly, you are not selling off the goose (house) that lays the golden eggs (rents). Just eating the eggs.

Not all of our rentals are in the self-directed IRA. There are a number I've bought with profits from homes I've flipped. Others I've bought with funds from a zero percent offer on a credit card. Yikes! Hey, it's cheap money. Others I've bought using private money. You will find the funds if you open your mind to possibilities.

"It's tangible, it's solid, it's beautiful. It's artistic, and I just love real estate."

Donald Trump

One of my greatest discoveries is the use of private money. You have opportunities to share. Here's one of my favorite deals. I bought a house from a remote full service wholesaler, paying him an assignment fee plus a modest fee to manage the renovation of the home. Then I offered an opportunity to fund this project to an individual who was earning next to nothing on some retirement funds. I had zero dollars in the project. I'd estimate between a few phone calls, emails, and a trip to Fed Ex, I put about three hours into this entire project. When the beautifully renovated home sold, I made a profit of nearly $20,000. The result was a happy wholesaler, a happy private money investor, and a happy me.

"People don't care how much you know until they know how much you care."

John C. Maxwell

Points to Ponder and Discuss:

If money was no object, what would you do?

How would your life be different?

Think back to a time in your life when money would have solved a problem. What was the consequence of not having the money needed?

Is money limiting you today?

Take five minutes and brainstorm all the potential resources you could use to find funds. Let your imagination run wild.

Act upon three of these ideas.

Money, money, money, money, money! (Yes, I hear Pink Floyd.)

You have to have money to make money. Everyone knows that. Right? WRONG!!

Real estate investing is such a beautiful thing. It has endless creative possibilities. It does not fall short of options in the way you fund your deals, or even whether you need funding at all.

No Money

Let's begin with no money. Everyone can do that, right? So you have no money. You may even have lousy credit. Or maybe you have money and good credit but you don't want to use it or risk losing it. So I recommend this again: begin with wholesaling.

When you wholesale a real estate transaction, you essentially act as a matchmaker. You find other investors who buy properties for cash. You talk to these fellows and see what they buy, where they buy, and how much they pay. Next, you essentially go shopping for them. Who doesn't like shopping? (Well, a few of you maybe, but I can help you with that issue another time.)

Once you know what your cash buyers want, you find highly motivated sellers with matching properties. These sellers might have their house listed on the MLS, in which case you will work with a real estate agent. These sellers might have them advertised as For Sale by Owner (FSBO), in which case you work with them directly. Or these sellers might not be waving any kind of flag saying "I want to sell my house" until you dig them up with your creative marketing. You make lots of offers, which costs nothing.

Once you have a property under contract (the owner has agreed to your price and you have a purchase agreement signed),

127

you essentially sell the deal to your cash buyer for a fee. Again, review Chapter 3 on wholesaling. As you can hopefully see, you can wholesale, wholesale, wholesale to make money, money, money.

Cash

Now you've wholesaled some houses and you have cash or maybe you are starting out with cash. Cash is king as the saying goes. You can make cash offers, get better deals, and then fix-and-flip or hold properties for cash flow for yourself.

Home Equity Line of Credit (HELOC)

You may have sources of cash you have never considered. For example, do you own your home? Is there any equity in it? I mean, is it worth more in today's market than the balance of your mortgage? If the answer is yes, then very possibly you could get a HELOC. This can be a very effective way to use your money to grow more money. If you took out a HELOC and were paying perhaps 4% interest and you used these funds to purchase, renovate, and resell a house to make a 10-20% profit, you are ahead of the game. Or maybe you use the funds to purchase a home as a rental and get a 15% return on your money. Again, you are ahead.

In fact, you have created what in the financial world is called "arbitrage", a profit based on the spread of two purchase prices, or in this case two rates of interest. Just toss that word around at your next REI Club meeting and you'll immediately sound like a savvy investor. I've used my HELOC over and over again for real estate investments. Make your money work for you!

Self-Directed Retirement Accounts

What about those retirement accounts that aren't performing so well? Oh sometimes the stock market is up, but then by the time you get done celebrating, it is down again. If you are anywhere near my age, you are starting to seriously think about whether you are going to have enough saved to live a comfortable life when you retire. You can self-direct the money in your IRA, 401(k), or even RRSP (Registered Retirement Savings Plan in Canada), and use these funds to invest in real estate.

Note that it is extremely important for you to consult an experienced administration company that understands the laws and tax implications of self-directed accounts. My husband and I have worked with such a company and purchased a number of homes with a self-directed IRA. Some sites you may want to research are:

www.checkbookira.com

www.accuplan.net

www.mountainwestira.com

www.trustetc.com

www.newdirectionira.com.

The appreciation those homes have experienced and the rent accumulated has more than replaced the big loss we took a few years back when the market tanked. We have reclaimed what the locust stole! The economy will continue to have its ups and downs, as will traditional savings, but people always need a place to live. Rents stay the same or even increase when home purchase prices drop. Isn't that interesting? So once you have a self-directed account collecting rent, you are pretty darn secure. That feels a lot better than being at the mercy of what the next election results may do to your savings.

Banks

Banks have tightened up their lending, but it is still possible to get traditional mortgages on investment properties. If your personal financial situation is good, you have the option of mortgaging your investment homes. Most banks follow the guidelines set by Freddie Mac and Fannie Mae, those big government agencies in the sky. Therefore, the number of traditional mortgages you can hold is limited. I'm not going to quote a number here, because these big guys are always changing things around.

A good mortgage broker is your best guide. You already know where you can find an excellent mortgage broker that understands working with investors – your local real estate investment club! I have used bank mortgages to purchase investment properties, renovate them, and resell them. The cost of getting the loan and paying it for a few months were greatly outweighed by the profit made in reselling the renovated home. You can also get a mortgage on a property you intend to hold as a rental. Just be sure you are netting more each month than the payment and other holding costs.

Small Community Banks or Credit Unions

There are literally tens of thousands of banks and credits unions in the U.S. The smaller financial institutions (those with one to five or so branches) have more options for investors. These local banks have portfolio loans that are kept in house, meaning they make their own loan decisions over muffins and tea. They are not bound to follow the guidelines set by Fannie Mae and Freddie Mac. So refreshing. Go in and talk to these nice people. See what the possibilities may be. One of our favorite techniques is to use small community banks to do a "no season" refinance on a property bought, renovated and rented, as discussed in Chapter 6 on holding properties.

Lines of Credit

Depending on your financial situation, traditional banks along with smaller local banks or credit unions may be willing to give you a personal or business line of credit. This is different than a mortgage or refinance. A line of credit establishes a maximum loan balance the bank will permit you to maintain. You can draw on this line of credit at any time, as long as you do not exceed the maximum set in the agreement. Make an appointment to discuss this possibility. In the worst case, you will find a free cup of coffee and biscuits to bring home to your dog.

Credit Cards

Yeah, the idea scared me at first, too, and I'm still not a big fan. However, I have used a cash advance on low or zero percent interest credit cards to purchase or renovate investment properties. Again, if the numbers work and you watch the calendar so you don't suddenly have credit card bills due at 29% interest, this can be an effective way to get cash for your real estate deals. Just don't tell your mom. She'll never understand.

Hard Money

That's a term that stumped me for quite a while when I was a brand spankin' new investor. What in the world? Are we talking about quarters and dimes? No. Hard money is a term used for legal usury. Ha! Again I jest. The fact is though; hard money is expensive. But if you run your numbers including the cost of getting a hard money loan, and you are still going to make a handsome profit, then there's no reason not to use it. Hard money lenders are professional lenders. Often they are also real estate investors.

When you seek a hard money loan, your personal cash and credit position is not what determines if you get the loan. The hard money lender is looking at the deal you want to fund. If it is a good solid deal, you will probably get the loan. The typical interest rate is 12-15% with three to five points (a point is one percent of the loan amount). Hard money lenders very seldom fund the entire deal. Generally, they will fund 75% of the purchase price, and they may or may not fund part or all of the renovation costs. So you still have to come up with some other funds. At these rates, you don't want a long-term loan. This type of loan is best used for flipping a house (purchase, renovate and resell). Six months is usually a good time frame for getting this done.

Another good use of hard money is as a short-term loan until you qualify for a more traditional loan or other funds become available. However, beware of additional costs, especially if you need to extend the loan. Remember, everything is negotiable. Whatever works for both parties can become an agreement. Try that with a traditional bank and see how far you get!

Private Money

Ah, just to see those words makes me smile. Let's read them again: Private money. Aaahh. Such a wonderful concept for all involved. Private money lenders are not professional lenders. Because of this, the SEC (Securities Exchange Commission) has some opinions, i.e., regulations. Please consult an attorney familiar with the SEC regulations to be sure you are doing this properly. Private lenders are just folks you know who could benefit from making a better return on their money. Who is that? Everyone you know!

My first private lender was my neighbor who had enough money sitting in her bank account earning 0.5% to fund an entire house and renovation. I have other lenders such as people I've met at real estate investment meetings, siblings of my friends, my accountant, etc. Just start talking about the opportunities you have and ears perk up. You are not asking for money! Did you notice I said to talk about the OPPORTUNITIES you have? As you become educated in real estate investment and gain experience, you will have an opportunity to share the wealth.

Warren Buffett said in a 2012 CNBC interview, "I'd buy up a couple hundred thousand single-family homes if I could." (What puzzles me about that famous quote is – well, he could!) Anyhow, if it's good enough for Warren, it's good enough for me, for you, and for those you know.

Once you have an interested party, you will present a particular opportunity to them. Be careful to only tell them what they want to hear to make a decision. The confused mind says no, so don't confuse them! Some people have accounting-type brains and want to see all the figures. Yikes, you may even need an Excel spreadsheet. Other people may just want to see pictures of the house and the neighborhood. Know your investor and share the information that will make them comfortable investing in your opportunity. This is another time to remember that everything is negotiable.

What kind of return are they looking for? How long of a term do they want? How frequently would they like interest payments? Would they like a debt arrangement where they get a fixed percent return no matter how profitable your deal is? Or perhaps they prefer to split the profit with you in an equity arrangement, but here their return fluctuates with the net profit of your deal.

Once you've decided all of this, have an attorney create a promissory note and mortgage or deed of trust to secure the investment with the property. These documents are filed with the county. You also name the investor in the insurance policy as the lien holder. It is about as risk-free an investment as possible. And you, my friend, are the one holding the goods.

 This private money thing sounds amazing, right? Would you like to hear a bit more?

Go to www.atimetoprofit.com/learn

"The world stands aside to let anyone pass who knows where he is going."

David Starr Jordan

Building Momentum –

Here are Some To-Do's:

Explore your Financial Options

- Look at your 401(k) and IRAs

- Find a self-directing custodian

- Look at your credit card limits including cash advances

- Find hard money lenders locally. Your REI club is a good start

- Make a list of everyone you know who may be interested in the opportunity to be a private money lender

- Determine if your home has the equity to qualify for a HELOC

- Meet with a several banks and discuss a line of credit

Chapter 9

Expose the Facts and Not Opinions: Market Conditions, Trends & Analysis

"Flaming enthusiasm, backed by horse sense and persistence, is the quality that most frequently makes for success."

Dale Carnegie

After doing a deal with a partner and splitting the profit, I understood the possibilities for wholesaling across the country. I realized my strong suit was getting good deals locked up. I learned to be comfortable talking to banks and negotiating deals that were attractive to buyers. All I needed was a rough idea of the repair costs and some comparable sold homes to figure out the home's ARV (After Repair Value) once it was fixed up. From there I could run numbers and make offers on any property across the country from the comfort of my own home. How cool is that?

I was able to get a home locked up in Murfreesboro outside of Nashville, TN. I was able to lock up the home for $70,000. Without a buyers list or a team in place in Nashville, I went to some networking sites for real estate investors and asked who wanted to split a deal. I found an awesome lady on www.deangraziosi.com, and she said she'd be happy to send it out to her buyers.

I asked her to advertise it for $80,000. That would get us $5,000 each profit. She was excited about the deal and sent out all the information right away. After just one day, she called saying she had a buyer who really wanted the property, but she was bummed because they only wanted to pay $76,000 for the property. She was happy for the opportunity and was willing to take only $1,000 profit and I could have the $5,000 profit I was hoping for. I told her she did half the work so she would get half the pay. We took $3,000 each in the $6,000 assignment.

It was one of the easiest deals I've ever done. I was able to do half the work – really less than half since I was able to focus on the part of the deal I was good at. I decided this was the way to go, and I wanted to do more. I was able to do deals in a few other states and expand my business through wholesaling with a partner in the local market.

"You always pass failure on the way to success."
Mickey Rooney

Once you are ready to leave your backyard, meaning you've done a few deals nearby so you have earned your dirty fingernails, now you can get a manicure and invest remotely in the most lucrative markets. What makes a market lucrative? That depends on your business strategy.

If you want to flip houses, you are going to want to find homes priced below market value in stable neighborhoods. When I decided to start investing in Cleveland, Ohio, the first thing I did was find an investor-friendly real estate agent. How? Believe it or not, this master agent came from a search on Facebook. (Never underestimate the power of social media for building your team.) I called him and asked if he worked with other investors. Not only did he work with others, but he had been investing himself for thirty years in Cleveland. He knew it all. Home run.

I had some definite ideas about where I wanted to invest. There were a few suburbs I knew from when I had lived there 20 years prior, and I was sure they would be ideal. My agent tolerated my thoughts and sent me listings, but he drew the line when I wanted to buy from this mountainous pile of homes. Here's a great analysis he taught me. (I learn so much from my team.)

He ran the number of houses under $40,000 available in two of the zip codes I liked. One zip code had 92 houses and the other had 102 houses. "Awesome!" I thought in blissful ignorance. Then he ran houses available under $40,000 in two zip codes he was recommending. One had seven, and the other had eleven. Slim pickings. That's the point! You want to invest in neighborhoods where the low-priced distressed property is the exception, not the norm. Oh. Then you have a good chance the home will retain its value. You could buy a house in these neighborhoods, renovate it, resell it at retail and make a healthy profit.

Renovating homes in areas with a large percentage of low-priced, distressed properties does not produce a profitable flip. It may, however, create a house with good rental potential for cash flow. There are lots and lots of neighborhoods around the country where you can achieve a positive cash flow as a rental but have very little equity in the home.

Personally, I like to have my cake and eat it too. (I could never understand why you would even want the cake if you couldn't eat it.) I only buy homes with a strong equity position and positive cash flow potential. That way, I have multiple exit strategies. If I ever want to sell one of my rentals, I know I will make enough money on it at any time to take a nice trip to Hawaii and then some. I may even eat some cake while I'm there. Hopefully coconut!

Points to Ponder and Discuss:

Think back to a time in your life when you allowed an assumption or stereotype to guide your decision-making.

What was the result? Would the outcome have been different had you researched the facts?

Have you ever not done something or not told someone about something you were interested in because you were worried about someone else's opinion or judgment?

How has this held you back from opening doors of opportunity?

Have you ever had to make a life-changing decision that was outside your comfort zone?

When you stepped out, what was the result?

Watching for Market Changes

When the real estate market crashed along with the economy in 2007-2008, most people were shocked. We just didn't see this coming. In hindsight there have been endless commentaries on what the signs were and how we should have done this or that. Yes, it's so much easier to be the couch quarterback after the fact.

So how can you tell when a market is changing? It is difficult to listen to the news because it always seems to discuss extreme examples. Drama sells so they're not going to do it any other way. Realtors have a tendency to get sucked into the water cooler gossip. Instead of relying on factual information, they have a tendency to relay whatever is the "hardest" story they can. For example, after the bottom of the market fell out and I was trying to get started in real estate, every agent told me I missed my window and that nothing was worth anything anymore.

When I make calls to new agents or to new markets looking to find a good agent, I get a completely different story now. Homes are not selling for discounts anymore, you can't get a good deal, and there is no inventory. Where were these agents waving a flag when the market was, as Goldilocks would say, "just right"?

In reality, there is no perfect time to invest in real estate. There is only now! There will always be opportunities. These opportunities will change or new opportunities will come to the forefront of the market, but there will always be opportunities to make money in real estate.

Right now is being called the Perfect Storm for the Flip. Home prices are finally coming back, solidly in some areas. There are also still opportunities to get good deals. So find a good deal in need of TLC and then, after you've worked your magic, you can sell it in the growing market for a nice profit.

From 2009 and on the market was primed for rentals. With foreclosures at an all-time high and home prices at the lowest they'd been in a decade, great deals were abundant. Also due to all the foreclosures and credit crunches, rentals were in strong demand. This allowed for landlord investors to get maximum cash flow and return on their investment.

However, that didn't mean you had to do one or the other during those time periods. In both of those varied markets there were investors looking for the right deal. If there are investors, or buyers, looking for the right deal, then there is always an opportunity to wholesale. And the bonus is you do not need credit or cash to make money wholesaling. Regardless of the market, you can make money.

Now to the meat and potatoes of finding out about the economy: How can you tell where it is and where it is trending? There are several key indicators that can give insight into the changes in the economy. First is the average days on market for an area. The second is market price changes for a set area. Finally, the overall economic condition for an area can often be tracked by the changes in the local unemployment rate. This is all good information, but how do you look it up?

First start with finding the average days on market. I find this to be the easiest of the three indicators since it is tracked by the MLS. Your Realtor should be able to pull the average days on market for homes of any size or style in a given area. Give your agent the criteria for the homes you're interested in, and they can pull for you the three-month average. From then on you can request this on a monthly basis to see which direction the market is trending. When the average days on market shrinks, the economy is often improving. This improvement usually correlates with decreasing inventory of available homes and the increase in home prices. When the average days on market increases, the economy is often declining. The decline can lead to an increase in home inventory and often price decreases.

One thing to note is that days on market, inventory, and prices can decline at varying times during the year. For example, between Halloween and tax return season the market will naturally slow. In contrast, during spring and summer months the market usually picks up due to the school year summer break. This natural break makes it easier for families to move and helps avoid the need to change schools during the school year.

The next factor is the home price index. Are home prices going up or are they going down? You can determine this by looking at your average days on market report. It can also include the average sales price for those homes. See how it is trending on a month to month basis. Once again you'll need to take into account any natural changes for your area.

To find out what the home price index is for your area of interest start with good old google. I search on google, "market price index Denver, CO." I scroll down the list of results until I find the Zillow page that offers Denver CO Home Prices & Home Values. I click on the link and it takes me to a page full of information. At the top right it will tell you the average home price and will give you the price change for the last year and a forecast for the upcoming year. I also want to look at the overall trend for the last several years. So I scroll down further until I get a chart for the last 10 years. Did it have a big drop around 2008 and 2009 and is it rebounding strongly now? This gives me a feel of how volatile the market prices are in that area.

The numbers here are usually the opposite from the average days on market. If the prices are increasing, days on market are usually going down along with available home inventory. The economy is usually looking up. However, do not speculate and purchase based on the increase in prices. As we learned previously, price increase can stop at any time. If prices are decreasing, days on market are usually increasing, and inventory has a tendency to increase as well.

Lastly, you can find out the overall economic condition for a city by looking up their unemployment rate. Unemployment shows you the overall health for a market. So where do you find out what the local unemployment rate is? You can find the unemployment rate on the Bureau of Labor and Statistics at www.bls.gov. Again this is a government site that has too much information to dig through most of the time.

To find your local area's unemployment rate go to the drop down Subject. Under the category of Unemployment, select State and Local Unemployment rates. This will give you the current (usually a month or two delayed) unemployment rate of each state on the right-hand side. If you follow that column down to the bottom, you'll see a map of the US and the ability to select a state under the heading Regional Resources. This will redirect you to the major metropolitan areas for that state. Select the one that meets your area best, and that will take you to the ten-year trend of unemployment rates for that area.

Once again you'll want to see where the area is trending. If unemployment rates are decreasing, then the economic condition for the area is usually improving. If the unemployment rates are increasing, then the area may be having some economic struggles.

No matter what the economic condition is for the area, you may want to do additional research before you plan to fix-and-flip or buy-and-hold. Look to see how varied the industry is for the area. Is there one major employer or are there a variety of employers in the community? If there is one main employer, then one company can make or break that community. If the employer grows it can bring additional jobs, but if they decline or decide to move locations, then that can dramatically change the economy of the community.

Also, look to see which companies may be looking to move to the area. Often visiting the local Chamber of Commerce can give you this information. Also, do not rule out a good educated Realtor or even your real estate investment club for information and local data.

Another useful site is www.city-data.com. Here you can learn more than you need to know about a certain city or zip code. Popular median priced zip codes are an effective way to pick your market. Go to www.trulia.com and select Local Info. On the next page, type in the county you are considering. A heat map will appear. Select sale price. Look at the areas in the median range. Those are the areas prime for investment. Next look below the map at the popular zip codes. Pick the most popular zip codes in the median priced areas and work in those markets. You can even go to www.listsource.com and see which of those zip codes have the most cash sales. That's where your investors are!

Be in the know. Do not simply listen to others to find out what is happening in a market. Trust but verify. I often trust others' opinions on what's happening in the market, but if I'm going to invest cash I need to verify their intel. Numbers do not lie, so make sure you are an educated investor and be on the cutting edge of the market changes.

"We simply attempt to be fearful when others are greedy and to be greedy when others are fearful."

Warren Buffett

Building Momentum –

Here are Some To-Do's:

- Obtain a three month DOM (Days on Market) report from your real estate agent

- Check the last six months to one-year price changes from the MLS and www.zillow.com

- Check the unemployment rate on www.bls.gov

- Use www.trulia.com to find the most popular median-priced zip codes

---

Chapter 10

Reveal the Lifestyle of Your Dreams: What's Your Niche?

"For better or worse, you must play your own little instrument in the orchestra of life."

Dale Carnegie

I spent twelve years as a piano teacher teaching countless kids how to count 1, 2, 3, 4. Was the little finger number 1 or 5? Which pedal do I use and can I pleeeze use it? I really want to play the song that goes "da da daa daa daaa a daa daa da daa daa... (That's Beethoven's Fur Elise if you don't recognize it) Heavens, not again! Jingle Bells, Silent Night (I did take a lot of pride in seeing little hands playing Christmas songs every year, parents teary-eyed in the audience, and then cookies - what's not to love?) Linus and Lucy, Clementi Sonatinas, Ughhh stop!

I really should not complain. I made very decent money. Sitting in my living room, refereeing homework in-between students, brewing lattes, and baking dinner all at the same time. God is good, and teaching piano treated my family well for over a decade.

Enter real estate investing. I had three years of moderate but progressive success in investing, leading up to teaching and coaching, when I finally decided to "Burn the Ships". The history goes that when Spanish Conquistador Cortez landed in Mexico, he had the ships burned. Yikes! No going back.

Now let me tell you what I did. The first year of real estate investing, I still taught piano "full time" i.e., about 30 students. Just how much brain energy let alone hours in the day could I muster? I did OK in investing. My second year I quit teaching altogether and focused on investing. Hmmm, I did better but not great. I got scared. I wasn't moving as fast as I had hoped I would, nor was I piling up stacks of money.

Did I say I got scared? So...... I'm going to admit this out loud in print. I got scared and took a few (five) piano students during year three of my investing career. I told everyone it was because I wanted to try out some new improvisation styles I had learned. That was part of the reason. The truth is that I got scared.

There I was. I had a great little pool of buy and holds. I had private money partners. I was flipping houses in multiple remote cities. I was teaching investment strategies. I was contributing to real estate websites. At long last, I stood up and got mad at myself. I went into the piano room and opened the cupboard stocked full of student piano books.

The nostalgia of looking through these books made my heart ache. The terror of really burning the ships scared the living daylights out of me. But I did it. I filled about ten double Trader Joe's paper bags full of student books. I gave them to my teacher friends, praying they would bless lives and foster music in more little minds and hands. It just wouldn't be me doing it. Then (and now) I walk boldly forward, unfettered by the temptation of the ships to return to the safety of the Motherland. I'm here in Investment Land for good. 100%.

Don' be foolish. Wear a life preserver - but burn the ships when you can.

 Real estate investing finally helped me reach the point where I could leave my J.O.B. I had previously enjoyed what I was doing and liked the idea of my career. However, once you start making money for yourself, you realize that how hard you work affects how much you make. Sadly, that usually isn't true when you work a job for a company. That being the case, I still might have stuck around anyway but there happened to be a management change. I no longer felt appreciated for my efforts, and thanks to real estate investing, I was able to leave. The key is that it was my choice, and I'm grateful for that every day.

So now I'm working full time on real estate, and I'm moving forward with every effort going to the benefit of my business, not to another company. When I left my job, however, I still needed to take into consideration other investments for my retirement. I no longer had a 401(k) that my employer and I were contributing to every month. Now it was up to me to keep that going. One option was to keep the money in the current 401(k) and let it slowly grow at 2% or so a year. In truth, the annual fees would probably negate any of my profit.

It was time to be a smart financial investor in addition to a smart real estate investor. So I took my 401(k) and rolled it over to a self-directed IRA. In addition to rolling it over to an IRA, I changed it to a Roth IRA. I had to pay taxes on all of it, but it was a good decision.

My thoughts were that if I paid taxes on a small amount, and then let it grow tax-free, I would be able to take it out tax-free during my retirement. The tax-free benefits are huge, especially since I do not think taxes are going to be less in the future. Chances are taxes are going to be much more, so I'll appreciate that tax-free situation. Also, since I'm working solely for myself, I have the ability to do a few more deals to pay those extra taxes that are due now.

Okay, so I've got my self-directed Roth IRA. Now what? I needed a way to get a good return on my money and have it grow at a hearty rate. I felt most comfortable in the real estate arena because it is something I understand. I didn't want to have to learn about the stock market or mutual funds because that would take away from my focus. So I thought about what my obstacles are as a real estate investor. The number one thing I came up with was getting enough money to do all of the deals I wanted to do. How can I use this to make a good profit for my IRA?

I started talking to real estate investors I knew and trusted – people I knew who were rocking and rolling in the market and could use a little more cash to get one more deal going. I found a partner in Minnesota who was happy to pay me 12% annual interest on my IRA. He said he would need the money for three to six months at a time. Sweet. That meant that I'd make 1% interest each month on my money. That's a great return, but even better, my money is backed by real estate. Again, that was something I knew, understood and felt comfortable with. A great return made me that smart financial investor I wanted to be, as well.

"Nothing is more difficult, and therefore more precious, than being able to decide."
                                                     Napoleon Bonaparte

Think of your life as a full bookshelf. You have a treasured new book that won't fit. You are going to have to remove an old book or two to make room.

What in your life can you eliminate to make a place for your dreams to become reality?

Are you a person who struggles to say "No"?

Think of a time you committed to more than you should have.

What did it cost you?

Did the benefits outweigh that cost or not?

Visualize your life as you want it to be twelve months from now. What talents do you possess to take you there?

What are you willing to sacrifice to live your ideal lifestyle?

What is Your Niche?

 Finding your niche in the vast world of real estate investment can take time. Be patient. You are going to have to try on a lot of different hats to see which one suits you best. Our recommendation is to begin to wholesale in your backyard. Remember, your backyard is anyplace you can drive back and forth to in a weekend. There are really good reasons for this. There is no risk, and you get to see the operations firsthand. Furthermore, it's a good idea to do several of the same types of deal before you branch out. That way you really understand the strategy. When you are ready to move on, you might select lease options, which are another great way to make money without using any of your own.

One obvious way to pick your niche is to analyze what options are open to you. Do you have cash? This could be savings or funds from a HELOC, a traditional mortgage, private money, etc. If the answer is yes, then you can branch out into flipping or holding properties. If the answer is no, then you will stay with "no money" strategies until you've earned enough to allow other options.

What's your background? All of our life experiences can be put to use in the field of real estate investment. Do you have experience in the construction field? If so, then you might have great value to another investor. Perhaps you team up and manage flipping properties. Is your expertise financial? You will probably be great at explaining opportunities to potential private money investors. Are you a stay-at-home mom like me? Then you have superhuman powers and can do anything you set your mind to! I joke, but seriously, don't underestimate the value your past life experiences bring to the table.

How much time and energy do you want to put into this? Are you a competitive, have-something-to-prove type of investor?

153

Then you are going to scale tall mountains of real estate success. You are driven, and will always desire to accomplish more. Are you more of a lifestyle investor? You want to earn enough to live the life you choose but still stop and have lunch with your kids or go away for the weekend. One is not better than the other. They are just different life choices. This clarification is going to help define your niche. Be honest with yourself.

What will ultimately define your niche is when something strikes just the right chord in you and gets you excited. More than excited, you will be determined. Confident and certain that you WILL. Jim Rohn said, "How long should you try? *Until.*" How long does a baby try to walk? Until. Not only will you try, you just will. How long will you pursue success in your niche? *Until.*

For me, when I heard about establishing a remote power team, it just lit that proverbial light bulb above my head. I left that event KNOWING I would establish a remote power team and own ten cash-flowing houses within the next twelve months. Period. No questions. None of this "it's too hard" business. I just did it UNTIL. The next thing that got the fire in my belly burning was when I learned about private money. I had never felt right asking for money.

I learned from my mentors that I had an opportunity, in fact, an obligation, to help people earn more on their savings. It became my mission. I have funded every deal in the last four years with funds from private investors. This is my niche, buying properties in remote cities where the numbers make great sense, flipping or holding and doing it all with private money. It gets me salivating just thinking about it. Or maybe it's the smell of the ham in the oven. Either way, with patience you will discover your niche and attack. Attack *until.* You'll feel giddy inside and help lots of people along the way.

"There is a vitality, a life force, an energy, a quickening, that is translated through you into action, and because there is only one of you in all time, this expression is unique."
Martha Graham

Building Momentum –

Here are Some To-Do's:

Spend some time soul searching

- Where are you right now?

- What are your life experiences and how can you put them to use?

- What do you love to do?

- Why are you doing this? Your "why" will help you find your niche.

- Where do you want to be in a year?

- How are you going to get there?

- Define what you need to succeed!

Chapter 11

Unleash Your True Potential: Goal Setting

"People are not lazy. They simply have impotent goals – that is, goals that do not inspire them.

Tony Robbins

"A goal is a dream with a deadline."

Napoleon Hill

 I've had a lot of great education to help speed my way to success in real estate investing and to reduce the number of my mistakes. I had an amazing mentor – a real "go getter", a highly successful thirty-something single man who lives and breathes real estate.

Despite my moderate, even respectable level of success, whenever I would think about this individual's success, I felt like a failure. I went around for probably a year feeling badly about myself because I wasn't achieving what this guy was. Then one day I woke up and said to myself, "Are you crazy? You are not him. Your life is not his life. Your goals are different than his. Your definition of success isn't the same. Dang lady, you are a success."

Man, that felt really good. I gave myself permission to be me – to still spend time with my kids, to walk my dog and even play a little piano, to be happy doing the amount of real estate I want to do, and to maintain my idea of balance in life. I'm a sixty-something married woman with four children. Why would I think I should mirror a thirty-something single man? I'll tell you why. The enemy wants to hold you down. He wants you to feel like a failure even when you are rolling in success. He wants to make you sad when there are a multitude of reasons to be happy. Don't put up with that. Be the unique blessing that you are.

"This above all: to thine own self be true, And it must follow, as the night the day, Thou canst not then be false to any man."
William Shakespeare

I was really slow to buy into goal setting. It just seemed like a needless thing to do. I mean, I would know when I'd accomplished something, right? Well, let me tell you a silly story about goals and walking in faith.

There was a rather prestigious conference at which I wanted to speak. (Yes, I'm one of those oddballs who actually loves public speaking.) It would be quite an honor and accomplishment to be asked. So I was writing my goals in January for the year. Nothing fancy mind you, just a spiral notebook and purple ink. I wrote, "Be asked to speak at ..."

A few weeks later I was shopping with my daughters and spotted a tee shirt that said, in big sequined letters, "VERY BIG DEAL." I loved it! That would be perfect to present in! The shirt was around thirty dollars. Having grown up very frugally with a carpenter father and house cleaning mother, I'm, well, kinda cheap. (I'm working on changing that.) So I didn't buy it. It nagged at me in the back of my mind for a month or two.

Then my daughters and I returned to the same store. There hanging on the front edge of the clearance rack, priced at $1.99, was my shirt! And only one of them! That is a God thing. Of course I bought it and hung it in my closet. Another few weeks went by, and, yep, it happened. I was asked to speak at the event. It was a wonderful moment when I walked up on stage. "A Very Big Deal" indeed. Put out there what you want. Write it. Speak it. Sing it. Pray it. It's not going to fall on deaf ears.

"Setting goals is the first step in turning the invisible into the visible."   *Tony Robbins*

Points to Ponder and Discuss:

Do you dare to dream?

Are you open to your dreams becoming reality?

Do you struggle to feel worthy of your dreams?

Do you remind yourself and the universe about what you want?

Think back to a time in your life when you wanted to achieve something: a new exercise routine, a new eating plan, spending more quality time with your family.

Did you tell someone about it? Did you have a friend do this with you and hold you accountable? If so, how did that help you?

What is scarier, staying where you are or achieving your dreams?

Is it failure that frightens you, or success?

Right now, say out loud what you want to achieve.

Do this daily!

Goal Setting

My Goal Focus

 I like to break down goals into a couple of categories (long term, short term, and specific tasks to achieve the goals)

Long-term goals can be anywhere from one to ten years, but they are usually five or more years. Ask yourself how you see your future and why is it you'd like to be successful in real estate.

Now short-term goals are usually the drivers for your day-to-day success. These are often a month or two, possibly up to a year or two. These are what push you to get going and do real estate investments. Knowing specifically what your short-term goal is will help you achieve your goals by breaking your days down into tasks. Tasks are what take you from doing (being busy) to accomplishing (doing deals)!

Okay, so what makes a goal a good goal? Well, it has to be important to you. If it isn't important to you, why would you work for it? What is going to motivate you to do those tasks? Often people think, "I guess my goal should be...." That's crazy. Make your goals have value.

You need to define **specific** goals. Make sure they are tangible and achievable. **Tangible** means they are measurable and you will know you have hit them when you get there. **Achievable** means they are something you can get to. While we may be able to get to $1 million in the first year, our life circumstances may make that unrealistic. So make sure your goals drive you, but don't set yourself up for failure

Your goals need to be **written down** and with you at all times. I don't care if it is a piece of paper you carry in your wallet or an app on your phone, but it should be with you at all times so you can see what you're fighting for even when it feels really hard and difficult.

Tell someone. This is the most powerful tool I've found to make me successful. If I tell someone what I'm working for, I'm that much more driven to make it happen. It is easy to let yourself down, but it is much harder to let someone else down. I love the example of a workout or diet buddy. You usually will make it to the gym at 6 a.m. if you're meeting someone there. If you are not, then you can easily hit the snooze button.

Give yourself some **visual aids**. The more you have reminders of your goals and what you can accomplish, the more you're motivated to make it happen. For visual aids I love writing on the mirrors in our bathroom with dry erase markers so that when we're brushing our teeth each day we are reminded of what we're working toward.

A vision board. This doesn't need to be anything fancy, just a corkboard where you can stick pictures, souvenirs, and notes that represent your goals. I have one in my bedroom, and add to it regularly.

All right. Let's break it down.

What truly makes people successful is working toward goals one day at a time. We all have some time in our day when we could squeeze in some real estate work. We just have to make ourselves do it.

To achieve my goals, I need to break down the tasks. I start by coming up with a dollar amount for each of my goals. I know everything is about money, right? It is something tangible. Then I brainstorm what I need to do to reach that goal. I just make a crazy long list of things that can get me there.

I'll give you an example. We wanted to take our extended family to Hawaii for a week. We calculated that the trip would cost $18,000 for all of us to go (including airfare, condos, food, fun and a few excursions). I had four months to raise the money to get everything taken care of. I also knew that I averaged $3,000 per deal and often had to make 30 offers to get one deal completed.

$18,000/$3,000 deal = 6 deals (above what I'm already doing)

I average 30 offers for each deal, so 30 x 6 deals = 180 offers

180 offers over 4 months 180/4 = 45 offers/month

If an average month is 4.5 weeks, then that's an additional 10 offers a week I need to make to reach my goal.

We now have our goals. What do we need to do each and every day to achieve them? What are the steps? How do I find those steps and start taking action?

First you have to commit to some self-discipline and promise to avoid procrastinating. These are very common for all of us, but they are two major things that keep us from achieving our goals. Additionally, the next major step is to avoid busy tasks and focus on Action Steps. Action Steps are items that move you that much closer to your goal.

Now you've committed to some discipline and will do what you said you'd do. Don't let yourself down by getting distracted.

Okay, I've committed. Now what?

- List all of the action steps that need to be accomplished to make that goal happen.
- Brainstorm any and all ideas that may help you accomplish your goal and move your business forward.

- Criticize your list. I know this sounds strange, but you need to evaluate what is truly going to get you results and what is just going to be busywork.
- Prioritize. Put first things first. What has to be done first? I like the Franklyn Covey Method for ranking things:
  - A (Urgent. Must happen today)
  - B (Important. Should happen soon)
  - C (Nice-To's. You'll get to it when you truly have time)

Schedule. Once you've prioritized, you rank the A's 1, 2, 3, 4, 5 then the B's 1, 2, 3, 4, 5 then the C's 1, 2, 3, 4, 5.

Now Follow your Plan. Start with A1 and build from there.

Reevaluate what's not getting done. Ask yourself why this is happening. Think long and hard about what is going on with you and what is holding you back. Is it that you don't feel you have enough information? Is it your fear of the unknown?

What I do is sit down every Sunday night and outline my week. What do I have to do every day, and what do I want to accomplish? Then I assign them to each day. For example, one day I might look at listings, one day I'd make offers, and one day I'd post ghost ads on the properties I had offered on.

Now I have to schedule around other requirements like picking up my son from school. Many of you have jobs so you have to schedule in the real estate piece. How do you schedule it in? Start with A1 in your first available spot, then A2, and so on.

What happens when a day flies by and you didn't do what you said because something came up? News Flash: Something always will come up. You may have heard the saying "Life gets in the way." Real estate investing now needs to become part of your life. Maybe this is what needs to be getting in the way.

So you missed a day. Now what? The normal reaction is to start again next week and promise to be better. How many of you have gone to the gym Monday and then missed Tuesday, so you decide that you will go again on Wednesday? Then you miss Wednesday and decide to start fresh on Monday. I'm sure that many have done this but might not admit it. You miss a day and work harder the next day to catch up on your A's. Don't tear yourself down because feeling badly won't help you tomorrow when you try to start again. Just realize that you're human and start again.

Now, what happens when you consciously say, "I don't feel like doing anything today, so I'm taking the day off." You just moved back the date of your goal. You have to realize you are consciously making a decision to postpone your success. If your "why" is strong enough, it should keep you from giving up.

In addition to delaying your success, when you choose to take a day off and choose to not do what you said you'd do, it won't be one day off. Chances are you'll wake up a week or a month later and realize time just flew by, and it will be like starting all over again. However, if that happens, GET BACK ON THE HORSE!

The keys to planning success are: Brainstorm, Evaluate, Prioritize, Schedule, and Follow Through!

"Obstacles are the things we see when we take our eyes off our goals."

Zig Ziglar

Building Momentum –

Here are Some To-Do's:

- Decide what goal-setting format you prefer

- Set Goals
  - Break them down
  - Decide on the necessary tasks
  - Assign the tasks
  - Review your goals and tasks weekly
  - Make appropriate adjustments

- Take Action.

- Enjoy your success along the way.

Chapter 12

Welcome a New You:
What's Next?

"Success is not the result of spontaneous combustion. You must set yourself on fire."

Reggie Leach

 When you are wholesaling, you don't need any money or credit. It's a beautiful thing. As your business evolves, you will surely want to expand the techniques you use. For me, nothing is quite as satisfying as a flip. There is the giant payday at the end, but beyond that is the pleasure of employing a lot of people in the process, creating from wreckage a beautiful home for a family, improving neighborhoods, and ultimately restoring America one house at a time. Have a big vision and you accomplish big things.

I had an experience that was life changing. I had purchased four houses. Some of them were in the final stages of renovation when I had the opportunity to teach a class in Cleveland and meet my Cleveland team for the first time. My contractor at the time assembled a team partially from an organization that trained former convicts to enter the work force. It was a decision I fully supported, but frankly, didn't think about much. It was his good deed.

I asked if I could take a picture of the team when I was in town because I wanted to use it for my social media marketing. They loved the idea more than I would have expected. About twenty workers gathered in one house and anxiously awaited my arrival. I strolled in 15 minutes late from what I thought was a more important meeting at the Chamber of Commerce.

Entering the house, I was immediately overwhelmed by upturned faces and downturned eyes, as if making eye contact would be too much. My contractor pointed out (not too discreetly) which workers came through the job training program. Folks of all ages, sizes, and colors were smiling shyly at me.

It was one of those moments when time stands still. I began to speak about what we were accomplishing together. The tears were hard to hold back for me and for many of them. My voice faltered as I thanked God for showing me His plan and how much grander and far stretching it was than mine. Be a vessel for good. You don't even have to understand it, just be willing to set sail.

"...if you have faith as small as a mustard seed, you can say to this mountain, 'Move from here to there' and it will move. Nothing will be impossible to you."
Matthew 17:20

Points to Ponder and Discuss:

What has this book done to help you evaluate your current life?

What are you committed to doing to achieve your bigger, better future?

Are you willing to take immediate massive action to make this a reality?

 *Do it today. Do it now.*

Ready, set, go!

What's Next?

This will be the launch of a new chapter in your life – a journey that wakes you up in the morning with a smile on your face. In fact, if you did the "To-Do's" as you read this book, you are already on your way. Even if you only opened up thoughts of possibility in your mind, you have started down the path. It is up to you now, but we are here to support you.

Does the thought of being your own boss excite you? How about living off of checks that appear in your mailbox? What about having the means to help your family? Is there a dream within you just begging to be set free?

This is your moment. Moments like this appear before us like flashes of lightening. Bright, loud, exciting, and then gone. Only the distant crack of thunder and a memory remain if you hesitate. Don't let that happen. Change is about momentum. It doesn't occur all at once. But this flash of lightening is shining on the path in front of you now. Yes, it is for you. It's open to anyone who dares to walk through the door.

Real estate investing is an opportunity to grab hold of your life and live on your terms. We'd like to help you. We've got your back. You need guidance and education to get this right. We did.

We have custom courses and even live events that can catapult your business success. We can get you started as a new investor by holding your hand through your first deal while you gain knowledge and confidence. If you are an experienced investor, let us train you to use the latest tools, techniques and secrets for our evolving market - to double, triple or totally explode your business. We have done both many, many times with massive success.

Go to www.atimetoprofit.com to see options that could be a perfect fit for you!

Let us help you help yourself. We would love to walk with you, hand-in-hand, down this path to success.

"God has given us two hands, one to receive with and the other to give with."

Billy Graham

Just Walk into the Sea

"Faith is taking the first step even when you don't see the whole staircase."

Martin Luther King, Jr.

One of my first real estate deals ended up being a lease option. I entered into the deal without quite knowing my exit strategy. At the time I didn't really even know what a lease option was. I knew it had something to do with renting a house for a while and then the tenants could buy it. Enough to get started I figured. So I ran an ad on Craigslist offering a lease option. Wouldn't you know it, the ad worked, and I had a family interested. Now what? I had no idea what to do. I reread a chapter in one of the books I had on real estate investment techniques, called a mentor, and got the help I needed. I worked with the family, getting more help along the way as necessary, and Ta-Da! I had a lease option under my belt.

You can't possible know everything before you move forward. Oh, get the basic knowledge, the education. Get a mentor or coach if you can. Then just move forward. Dare to go through the door you see in front of you. Dare to follow the light you see on your path.

Here's a Bible story I think about a lot. Moses is called upon to lead the Israelites to freedom from Egypt after generations of bondage. The Pharaoh is not easily persuaded to free the people. Moses has to plead with the Pharaoh over and over again. After some help from God in the form of frogs, lice, locusts, storms of fire, boils and a bloody river, Pharaoh succumbs and tells Moses to leave with his people. So along marches Moses and thousands of families. Men, women, children, babies, cattle by the thousands.

Suddenly he realizes the Egyptians are chasing him. The sound of the hooves of approaching warrior horses is getting frighteningly loud. Moses moves along with haste, but he can only push the masses so fast. Now what! What can that be? There's the Red Sea in front of him. Enemies pressing from behind and a major obstacle in front. Sound like life to you? What to do? Retreating is not an option. Seemingly, neither is moving forward.

Moses listens to the Still Small Voice, takes courage, believes and makes his move. Moses, instructed by God, holds a rod up above the water all through the night. It didn't seem to make any logical sense, but he obeyed. I'm guessing Moses stepped into the water, filled with fear and confidence at the same time, ventured maybe nose deep, before the water started to part. But part it did! The Red Sea opened miraculously before the Israelites. However, this miracle took courage. This miracle took decisive action. This miracle took persistence and moving forward beyond all that appeared reasonable. The Israelites escaped across to the bare ground. The pursuing enemy was drowned as the water surged over the briefly opened path.

You have a way of escape. You have freedom in front of you. You have paths opening for you. You must take the courage to go down them, one step at a time.

Made in the USA
Lexington, KY
10 December 2017